# JOB INTERVIEW QUESTIONS AND ANSWERS

*The Complete Process for Interview Preparation! Speaking Skills and Body Language for Winning Interview + 35 Powerful Interview Questions and Answers + WORKBOOK*

# Jordan Smith

*I have had my share of job interviews over the years. Some went okay. Some were complete failures. This book is dedicated to all of those of us who have bombed that all-important interview. This book will help you and remind you that you can do it. You can ace that interview and snag that job! Good luck to you all!*

Job Interview Questions and Answers: The Complete Process for Interview Preparation! Speaking Skills and Body Language for Winning Interview + 35 Powerful Questions and Answers + WORKBOOK Copyright © 2019 by Jordan Smith. All Rights Reserved.

All rights reserved. No part of this book may be reproduced in any form or by any electronic or mechanical means including information storage and retrieval systems, without permission in writing from the author. The only exception is by a reviewer, who may quote short excerpts in a review.

# CONTENTS

Introduction .................................................................. 7
**Part One** ................................................................. 13
The Pre-Interview ...................................................... 15
The First Impression ................................................. 25
Clothing ..................................................................... 29
Body Language .......................................................... 39
Speaking Skills .......................................................... 45
Know the Company ................................................... 51
Types of Interviews ................................................... 59
Tailoring Your Interview ........................................... 73
Taking a Practice Drive ............................................. 81
The Follow Up ........................................................... 85
Job Interview No-Nos ................................................ 93
**Part Two** ................................................................ 97
35 Interview Questions and Answers ......................... 99
**Part Three** ........................................................... 149
Interview #1 ............................................................. 153
Interview #2 ............................................................. 163

Interview #3 .................................................. 175
**The Workbook** .......................................... 181
In Conclusion ............................................. 195
**Bonus Content** ......................................... 197

# INTRODUCTION

Are you tired of going to interview after interview but never getting your dream job? This is why you need this book. After working in Human Resources for ten years, I have learned a few things and want to share them with you so you can get the job you most desire. There were people I had to interview who had it all together when they arrived. They were the whole package. They were the ones I hired.

Then there were the opposites. Some people looked like they just walked in from the barn, and they smelled like it too. I thought that was bad enough, but then they opened their mouths to speak. Some slurred their words as if trying to speak around a mouthful of gumballs. Some would give one word answers. Some would speak rather disrespectfully and not appropriate for the interview in which they hoped would result in employment.

Yes, there are common sense issues, but you would be surprised at the number of people who don't pay attention to all of those little details. If you want to work in a customer based job, open your eyes as a consumer. When you go to a restaurant take note of what your waiter or waitress looks like. Are they dressed neatly? Are their fingernails clean? Who wants to eat food that has been prepared or served by a dirty individual? Are they smiling and happy to see you? Or are they grumpy and appear to want to be anywhere but where they are? It may seem silly, but there are so many simple things like this that people overlook when preparing for a job interview. We will cover them all.

This book will help you with your interview from start to finish. There are things you need to take care of before you leave your house and show up at the office. In this book there will be much discussion on what to say, how to act, and what to bring to your interview. I will give sample interview questions, what the interviewer is looking for, and ideas of how you can answer them. In the last part of the book will be even more sample questions where you can write out answers for yourself to better help you prepare for the interview. The better prepared you feel, the better you will perform in the moment.

Other books might promise to help you by giving you questions that potential employers might ask and some sort of answers. The problem is that not everyone can answer questions the same way. We all have different employment experiences. We aren't all the same age. This book will not only give you some of the most popular interview questions but help you answer them personally and in a way that catches the ear of the interviewer and makes them give you a second thought instead of tossing your application and resume in the slush pile.

You may find that some of the ideas here may seem like common sense. They are if you have attended your share of interviews; however, I hope to reach a younger crowd as well who may never have had an interview. This book covers EVERYTHING you need to know before, during, and after an interview. Maybe there are some things you have never thought of doing before an interview. I assure you this book covers it all and will give you new ideas to face the interview process with confidence.

There are many books on the market that promise to help people get a job. Those books only offer up some questions with cookie cutter answers. Well, we are not cookie cutter people. This book is designed to help you tailor your answers to you. With that being said, this book is not a magic book that if you read it cover to cover one time, all your employment dreams will come true. You have to study the questions and answers. You have to practice. You have to put forth the effort. Your effort combined with this book will be a winning combination.

This book is divided into three parts. The first part will tell you everything you need to know to prepare for the interview. The second part will contain some of those most often asked questions along with answers you can tailor to meet your needs and job experiences. The third will give sample interviews and also a workbook to record your own answers to example questions.

I suggest reading through the book all at once at first. Then read it again, grabbing a highlighter and marking everything you want to take note of or need to personally work on. When you get to Part Two, really study all the questions. Make notes beside them. Think about how you could reword the answers to make them fit you and your job experiences and life situations. When you reach Part Three, again study the questions and answer, especially taking note of why the interviewer is asking the questions. When you know the reasoning behind the questions, that will help you verbalize a more appropriate answer.

The purpose of this book is to help you gain confidence when attending an interview, whether it is a phone interview, an online interview, in person, one on one, or with a group. If you have gone to multiple interviews with no results, then you need to make sure you read this book and put it to use before your next one. This winning combination will help you seal the deal and start receiving paychecks.

***Thanks again for choosing this book, make sure to leave a short review on Amazon if you enjoy it, I'd really love to hear your thoughts.***

# PART ONE

*What to Know Before You Go*

**Chapter One**

# THE PRE-INTERVIEW

*"The most important tool you have on a resume is language."*
— *Jay Samit*

You can't get an interview without first submitting a resume. Consider the resume your pre-interview when applying for a job. You need to prepare a resume that will make you stand out from the crowd. When looking at a resume, a potential employer will not see your face, hear you speak, or be able to watch your body language, but they can still read a lot through this every important piece of paper.

In general, keep your resume relatively short. You do not need more than a page or two. The hiring manager wants to see what is relevant to the job, not your entire life's history. Keep it concise and easy to read.

## Types of Resumes

There are several types of resumes and you will have to decide which one is best for you and the job for which you are applying. Your resume choices are targeted, functional, chronological, or a combination of the three.

The targeted resume is going to do just as it sounds. It is going to zero in on your experiences that have to do specifically with the job for which you are applying. On the targeted resume you essentially want to give a list of your qualifications that make you the perfect fit for this job. You will still list your previous employers, but you will focus on what the employer is looking for for the position that they have available.

A chronological resume is just as it sounds as well. You would work backward listing your most recent positions and give a little bit of information about each one including the length of time you worked there and what your job requirements were. Start with your most recent and go back to two to three jobs. It is not necessary to list every job you have ever had, especially if you have been in the job force for many years.

A functional resume is a little bit different in that it focuses on what your strengths are and the experiences you have had on the job. This is an ideal resume for those who are looking to change careers after working in one field for a length of time. The jobs you held will probably not have comparisons to the job that you are trying to get. This would also be a good type of resume for young people who do not have a lot of job related work experience. Focus on your talents that fit the position.

If you want to combine different aspects of the three above resumes that is fine too. Just make sure to keep it well organized, clear, and concise.

## What to Include on Your Resume

Of course, you want to include your job history on your resume, but you do not need to include every job you have ever had, especially if you have been in the workforce for many years. If this is the case, include your last three or four jobs. That should be sufficient particularly if the time period of those few jobs covers 10 to 20 years.

On the other hand, if you have had an exorbitant number of jobs in the last few years, you will want to be more selective. You do not want the hiring manager to see a long list and wonder why you have not been able to hold down a job for more than a few months at a time. That's a red flag for them.

If you are a young person and new to the job world, you will want to include as much as you can without cluttering up your resume. A future employer will not necessarily be looking at your past experience, but at the fact that you are a hard worker. Jobs young people can add include babysitting, yard work, or working in a family owned business. You may also want to include extra-curricular activities such as sports, music, clubs at school, and any volunteering you have done. This gives the impression that you are well-rounded and hard working.

## Formatting Your Resume

There are plenty of templates either already on your computer or that you can download for free online. Use a template if you are unsure of your formatting abilities.

One of the formatting factors you want to keep in mind is the font. An excessively large font is not necessary. In fact, it's annoying. A normal size 12 font is best. Another factor you want to remember is that you do not want to use fancy fonts. Some of them may look nice but can be very difficult to read, especially if someone has to look at resume after resume. Choose a font that is clear and easy to read, such as Times New Roman, Calibri, or Arial.

It is also not necessary to add a lot of extra formatting to your resume. Bullets, italics, bolds, etc. should only be used for section headings and any information (be very selective) you want to stand out of your resume.

## Keywords

One of the new aspects of job hunting today is the process by which companies look at resumes. Many of them use ATS software (Applicant Tracking Software). These programs can scan digital resumes and look for keywords that are specific to a particular job description. Since a lot of companies use this software, it is imperative that you research the position for which you are applying and know what words would stand out on your resume.

You want to include any keywords that promote your experiences and skills that match that job description. If you are unsure what keywords to use, examine the job posting a little more closely. Use words that they use. Use job specific terminology.

Keep in mind that this software is automatic and that sometimes a human pair of eyes will never see your resume if it does not pass the ATS test. There is a line you can cross however when it comes to using too many keywords. An ATS system will pass on your resume if there are too many keywords as it will flag it as spam.

## Perk Up Your Resume

Take another look at your resume before completing it, especially looking at the job descriptions you included. Think of more creative ways to say what you did at previous jobs. If you were a waiter or waitress, do not just say you "waited tables." Give a little more information. Write, "I was responsible for meeting customers' needs at 15 tables each night."

You can also choose words that have a little more meaning behind them. Make use of an online Thesaurus. Instead of saying you "painted" something, use the word "decorated." It gives a different impact.

If you have any unique skills that you believe would help cement your application being given a second look, make sure to include that information. Again look at what the job description is from the company and think about your skills that could take that job to the next level.

Be careful when dressing up your resume that you do not make an impression you do not intend to make or cannot live up to. If your resume is too bizarre, it will be noticed and tossed. Be realistic and truthful.

## Contact Information

Do not forget to add your contact information to the top of your resume. This is the only way a potential employer will have to get a hold of you if they would like to speak further. Again, use a font and a size that is easy to read. You can actually make the font a little larger for the header of your resume. State your full name, physical address, phone number, and email address.

After sending in your resume, make sure you check those forms of communication regularly. They cannot call you in for that face to face interview if you do not respond to them when they reach out to you.

## References

References are a very small, but extremely important part of your resume. You may want to change these references depending on the jobs for which you are applying. Different friends and previous coworkers may have different viewpoints of you and your work ethic depending on your past work relationships. If you are applying for a manager's position with a construction company, maybe one of your references could be the neighbor you built a deck for. They can definitely speak about their experience working with you as well as the quality of your work.

Remember to ask permission from those who you want to add to your resume as references. You do not want them to be surprised, and not in a good way, when someone calls asking questions about you. When you ask permission, this also alerts them to the fact that they might be getting a call, leaving them time to prepare as to what to say.

## Facial Recognition

There is one little embellishment you can add to your resume to make yours stand out. You can add a small (very small) head shot of yourself to the head of your document. If you decide to add this, make sure it is a professional looking photo, not a photo of you in a bathing suit at the beach with a beer in your hand. A small photo will help give facial recognition to whoever is looking at your resume. Your face may stick in their memory as someone they would like to speak to further.

Remember, small. Do not go crazy with the picture as that will have the opposite effect and land your resume in the trash.

## Proofing Your Resume

Do not neglect to look over your resume before you send it out. Once you have completed your resume, it is best to let it sit untouched for several days. This way when you do go back to look at it you will not skim over errors and you will be a little bit more objective in reading what you wrote. You can double check to make sure that you added all the necessary information while eliminating anything that might look derogatory toward you. It might also be a good idea to have somebody else look over your resume to make sure that everything is correct and that all the information is clearly stated.

## Chapter Two

# THE FIRST IMPRESSION

*"You never get a second chance to make a first impression."*
— *Will Rogers*

This section assumes your application and resume have been looked over by a potential employer and yours looks promising enough that they called you to come in for an interview. Take a deep breath. You can do a lot ahead of time to prepare yourself. The more confident you are, the less nervous you will need to be.

But there is one aspect of job hunting that you need to put a considerable amount of thought into. What do you want to do with the rest of your life? Do not look at a job as temporary. Do not think of it as a "for now" job. Really think about what it is you want to do for a living. What would be your dream job? That job that you would do even if you were not getting paid? That is where you need to start. When you are passionate about what you want to do, you will be amazed at the difference in your interviews. You will be excited about getting the job. Your attitude will not be ho-hum, "I need a paycheck" conversations. When something is important to you, it shows all over your face, in your attitude, in the words you speak, and how you speak them. So, think about what you want to do and be happy earning a paycheck, and then go for it. Go all out and see the difference it makes.

Several areas you can look at and take in hand before you go include your clothing, your body language, your speech, researching the company, taking a drive to where your interview will take place, and the different types of interviews you may face.

Getting all of these aspects of your interview under control before you even leave for it will give you an extra boost of confidence. That confidence may help your interview performance and increase your chances of being offered a position.

## Chapter Three

# CLOTHING

*"Clothes make the man. Naked people have little or no influence on society."*— Mark Twain

Always wear appropriate clothing for an interview. Keep in mind that your physical appearance is the very first impression you will make on any person, including a potential employer. Your appearance is extremely important. Overdress if necessary. Do not ever underdress. The one who is dressed in a suit and tie or a tailored dress and heels will automatically make a better first impression than someone who comes in wearing dirty jeans and sneakers. How you take care of yourself will ultimately reflect and how you will take care of things within a company.

Is your interview at a fast food restaurant or a Fortune 500 company? Does it really matter? If you want to knock the socks off your interviewer right away, dress properly. Consider the company with whom you are interviewing. Research the company to see if there is a dress code. If there is, follow that dress code for your interview. It may be a little difficult for you to find a dress code outlined somewhere until you are hired and receive an employee handbook, if there is one. However, you can still examine their website and even social media sites to see what people there are wearing.

## What to Wear

Business casual is okay for a fast food restaurant or maybe a job where you would be working outside, such as with surveying or construction. However, if you are applying for a job at an office, unless otherwise told, wear a suit and tie if you are a man or a dress if you are a woman. Women can also wear pant suits. Heels or flats are fine, but do not wear open-toed shoes.

If casual dress is appropriate, choose dark colored blue or black pants (this could include jeans, but not recommended) and a collared shirt, such as a button down or a polo. Never wear open-toed shoes or sneakers no matter the clothing style you choose.

When you choose what to wear, think about what looks good on you, especially with colors. Try on different shades of clothing and see what makes you look healthy and strong. Leave the clothes that make you look pale and sickly in the closet. If you are unsure of what to wear, choose dark colors. Black or navy blue looks good on most complexions. Be careful not to look like you are going to a funeral wearing all black, though. Add a pop of color with a feminine blouse or scarf for women or a colored tie for men.

Think about the season or time of year and choose clothes appropriate for that as well. You want to wear something comfortable. Going into a job interview in the winter wearing a sundress and goosebumps is not ideal. Neither is walking into an interview sweating because you chose inappropriate clothing for the weather. If it is summer, think about air conditioning. If you have a tendency to be cold in air conditioning, think layering when choosing clothing. A sweater that you can easily put on or take off is a good idea. When you go into an interview and are uncomfortable because of your clothing, you will more than likely be distracted and will not be able to put your best foot forward.

Try your clothes on to make sure they fit properly. Nothing should be too tight across the chest, leaving gaps in the buttons. Long sleeves should reach all the way down to the wrists. The hems of pants should reach the tops of shoes but not be so long you step on them or trip over them.

Ladies should be careful about wearing clothes that are too revealing. While the truth is that some men may enjoy revealing clothing, others do not. You want to show your potential future employer that you think more of yourself than to stoop to taking questionable actions to obtain a job. You do not want to give the wrong impression. Remember, professional is always best.

Another tip would be to examine clothing closely, especially if you have not purchased something new for the interview. Look for any snags or tears. Make sure there are no stains. To more clearly see flaws, examine your clothing out in the sunlight. Artificial or low lights, such as in a home, do not always allow you to see everything.

To be sure your clothing is wrinkle free iron it the evening before your interview. If you are not a fan of ironing, take your clothing to a dry cleaner and have them take care of it for you. It is usually less than $10 to have an outfit cleaned and pressed. Showing up for your interview with a pristine appearance is well worth that cost.

## Other Considerations

Jewelry should be kept to a minimum. If you must wear jewelry, wear something that is low key and not too big or flashy. Stick with discreet earrings and a necklace and leave the jangling bracelets at home.

Your hair is something else to consider before that all-important job interview. For men, if it's time for a cut, get one. Do not enter the interview room with everything looking great except for that shaggy hair on your head. For ladies, make sure your hair is done nicely. No messy buns. Some companies, especially those in food service, require hair to be tied up and not hanging loosely. If that is the case with your interview, do your hair in an appropriate manner.

After shave and perfume are also ways you can make a quick impression. These things are not bad...in small doses. Do not apply so much after shave or perfume that people can smell you before you arrive. Less is definitely more in this case.

Take a look at your hands a day or so before the interview. If your nails are looking a little scraggly, get a manicure. This goes for both women and men. Nails that are neatly trimmed and polished may not necessarily be noticed, but a hiring manager will definitely take notice of dirty, broken nails and chipped nail polish when shaking your hand. As a woman, if you decide to use colored nail polish, choose a lighter, less bold color. Your nails are not being interviewed. You want the interviewer to see you, not the neon green nail polish that matched yesterday's outfit.

A couple more areas that ladies need to take into account that men do not include pantyhose and purses. Some women prefer pantyhose, some do not. If you do not like wearing them and your legs don't look the best, maybe a pant suit would be a better option for your interview attire. If you do prefer covering your legs, stick with a neutral or dark (black or navy) color for stockings. As far as purses, choose something small and professional looking. If you plan on carrying a messenger bag or something with a portfolio in it, a purse is not necessary at all. Your portfolio bag will probably be large enough to keep your phone and keys in as well.

## Definite Nos

There are some definite items to not bring to or show during your interview. If you have a lot of piercings, maybe leave some of those at home. Piercings all over the body do not look professional and may turn the hiring manager off, especially tongue piercings. These piercings make it difficult for a person to speak. That is not the impression you want to make.

Tattoos are not loved by all companies, unless you are interviewing for a job as a tattoo artist. If you have a lot, cover as many of them up as possible for a more professional appearance.

Another point to keep in mind is to not bring anything extra to the interview. No gum. No cups of coffee or giant sodas. These can be distracting and will look unprofessional. If you feel it's necessary, pop a mint into your mouth shortly before walking into the interview, and it will dissolve in a few minutes. Nothing else.

If you do take your phone into the interview, leave it in your purse or bag and make sure it is turned off, or at least the volume and vibration are turned off so it will not be distracting to you or to the interviewer.

As stated before, it is better to overdress instead of underdress. You can always ask the interviewer if there is a dress code for the company. If you take care of yourself, and a potential employer can see that, they will assume you will take care of their company as well. No matter what you are considering putting on from your head to your toes, think about what a professional would wear and you will not go wrong. Sloppy never wins the job.

## In Summary

- Dress for the part
- Keep extras (jewelry, drinks, bags) to a minimum
- Pamper yourself beforehand by getting a haircut and a manicure

- Don't go overboard with perfume or cologne
- Cover things you don't want to be seen (tattoos, piercings, etc.)
- Overdress, never underdress
- Prepare clothing ahead of time

## Chapter Four

# BODY LANGUAGE

*"Don't underestimate the importance of body language!" - Ursula*

Your body language can say a lot about you as well; some of those things you probably wish no one would pick up on, especially a potential employer. Think about how you carry yourself. Watch yourself walk in front of a mirror. You want to look confident, but you do not want to look cocky. Do not walk into the interview as if you plan on taking over the interviewer's job followed by the company itself.

Even before you get into the interview, sit with confidence while waiting. While the hiring manager who is interviewing you may not be present in the room, there are other employees who may be keeping an eye on you.

## Walk Confidently

Walk with confidence into the room. If you are going to carry a portfolio or other type of bag, hold it in your left hand so you can easily reach out to shake the interviewer's hand with your right. The handshake tells the hiring manager a lot about you. You want to shake firmly, but not too hard and definitely not too soft even if you are a woman.

If you have to stand for a moment, stand up straight with your arms at your sides or with your hands folded in front of you. Do not slouch, lean against a wall, or put your foot up on the rung of a chair nearby. You never want to give the impression of being lazy or too tired to even stand for a minute or two.

Smile. Do not have a grumpy look on your face. If your face is one that has a tendency to look grumpy, like mine, practice in front of the mirror before your interview to make sure you show that you are happy to be there.

## Sitting Posture

Sit when asked. Sit up straight. Slouching screams of laziness, and no employer wants to hire someone who is lazy. The type of chair can determine how you sit. If it is a straight, hardback chair, sitting back is not an issue; however, if it is a more comfortable type of chair, you may want to sit forward a little keeping in mind that some comfortable chairs can be hard to get out of. You do not want to leave a last impression in the interviewer's mind of you not being able to get out of the chair gracefully. Wherever you sit, you want your sitting posture to show that you are interested and excited about the job. Again, set your portfolio or larger bag on the floor to your left. Place smaller folders either on the table in front of you or on your lap.

When sitting, place your hands in your lap or on the arms of the chair, whatever is comfortable for you, but also professional looking. Again, your choice will depend on the chair. Unfortunately, you will not know that until you get into the interview. Never cross your arms over your chest. That speaks of indifference or boredom, which are never good attitudes to portray when being interviewed.

Crossing your legs is not usually a good idea either. That forces you to sit farther back in the chair, giving that bored/indifferent/don't care attitude. Besides, if the interview lasts any length of time, you may need to switch legs due to one falling asleep. Any type of fidgeting can be distracting or send a negative message that you are not trying to send.

## Look Them in the Eye

Make eye contact. When you make eye contact, it not only shows confidence, it shows that you are listening to what the other person has to say. The interviewer wants to know you are listening and will not want to waste his or her time with you if they do not feel that you are there completely. Even if you have a lot going on in your life and you are desperate for a job, do not let the things outside your interview become an issue during your interview. A good rule of thumb is to use eye contact as if you were speaking to a friend. Your eyes can wander around the room a bit, but make sure to keep that contact when either you or the interviewer is speaking.

If you have a tendency to talk with your hands, do not think that is a bad thing. You do not want to go overboard or make large, animated gestures, but simple movements of the hands are okay. If you know you normally talk with your hands and try to curtail that during your interview, you may end up looking awkward, not knowing exactly what to do with yourself, and the impact will not be what you are aiming for.

## Watch Those Nervous Habits

Be careful of any nervous habits you may have. When some people are nervous they make crack their knuckles or play with their hair. If you do a practice interview with someone before the actual interview, they might be able to spot a couple of these things and point them out. If you are aware of them, you can change your body language. Fidgeting, nail biting, and foot tapping can also be signs of nerves or boredom. Neither are impressions you want to leave.

## Leave Confidently

Upon completion of the interview, how you leave is just as important as how you enter. Calmly gather up any belongings that you may have pulled out of your portfolio, stand smoothly (which should be easy if you are sitting on the edge of a chair with your feet flat on the floor in front of you), and shake hands with the interviewer. If you have been in an interview with a group, it might be awkward to go around the room shaking hands with everyone. Instead, nod your head and make eye contact with each one to show them your appreciation of their time.

## In Summary

- Be Confident, but not cocky
- Sit up straight
- Make eye contact
- Be mindful of your nervous habits
- Walk out confidently, own that interview

## Chapter Five

# SPEAKING SKILLS

*"The quality of your communication determines the size of your result."— Meir Ezra*

How you speak during your interview is one of the most important aspects you need to perfect. Speak clearly. You want to make sure you are heard, but you do not want to shout, either. If you are interviewing one on one in a small office room, your voice will not have too far to carry. If you are in a group interview or in a warehouse type of setting, you may need to speak a little louder to be heard.

## Thinking Before Speaking is Wise

When an interviewer asks a question, take a moment to consider it before speaking. You want to give your brain time to think before your mouth reacts. More often than not we speak first and think later. In an interview, you do not want to say words you cannot take back. You want to show that you have good communication skills, which are imperative to any job, whether a warehouse, fast food restaurant, or corporate office. It is hard to fake your way through proper communication, so this is a huge part of your interview and plays a large part in determining whether you are hired for the job or not.

## What to Be

Be yourself. Do not be afraid to let your personality shine a little bit, but do not go overboard. If you have a tendency to be sarcastic in conversation with your friends and family, leave that at home. Sarcasm has no place in the job interview. Talking about yourself is not a bad thing, in fact, you will more than likely be asked to tell a little bit about yourself. This is definitely something you want to consider beforehand. Think about the job for which you are applying and state what will help solidify that you are the right person for it. If there is any doubt about what you should or should not say, think about whether it is professional or not. If it does not sound professional, then do not say it. Be relevant to the job. Be you. Be original.

## Watch Out for Colloquialisms

Do not speak too casually, again, as if you were out for pizza with your friends. Also, try not to use Uhhh or Ummm. Always use "yes" and "no" over "yeah" and "nah." This is where taking the time to think before speaking will be greatly beneficial to you.

Discuss your skills that are pertinent to the job. If you have had leadership experience anywhere and are applying for a manager's position, let the interviewer know. If you are applying for a job that works with businesses overseas, state that you know more than one language.

## Honesty is the Best Policy

While it would not be hard at all to overstate your qualities, it is never a good idea. If you say you are proficient in a specific computer program, make sure you are. It will only backfire on you later if the company hires you and finds out you were less than honest in your interview. This frustrates companies and leaves them without adequate employees to do the necessary work. If you have a little knowledge about something, say so. Tell the interviewer that you are not afraid to learn new things and that you are willing to be taught. An employer would much rather hire someone they know that needs a little training than hire someone they think is perfectly capable only to find out that is not the case. Be honest.

## Be Clear. Be Concise. Be Positive.

When answering a question be sure to speak clearly and concisely. Say everything you need to say with as few words as possible. If you start getting long winded in your answers, you may not give the effect you are hoping for.

Be positive with whatever you say. Most statements, even ones with negative connotations, can be said in a positive manner. Do not say that you have had multiple interviews and no one is calling you back. Instead, say that you are looking for the perfect job for you to help fulfill a company's need.

# In Summary

- Give answers some thought
- Be yourself
- Speak clearly and properly
- Always be honest about yourself and your abilities
- Be positive

## Chapter Six

# KNOW THE COMPANY

*"Without ambition one starts nothing. Without work one finishes nothing. The prize will not be sent to you. You have to win it."*
— *Ralph Waldo Emerson*

Do some research on the company with whom you are interviewing. It may help you decide what to say and what not to say during your interview. Also, knowing a little more about the company will help you decide if it is someplace you really want to work or not. Find out what the company expects out of their employees, especially as far as attendance and work ethic. If you know someone who currently works for or has worked for the company in the past, ask them questions about their experience working there. Did they love it? Did they hate it? What exactly did they love or hate? Keep an open mind when speaking to past and current employees; some of their problems may be personal and not company-wide. It could also be that the job is just not a great fit for them but they continue to work there because they need the money.

So, how are you supposed to find out all this information? There are several ways to research the company to determine whether it is a good fit for you as a person and as an employee. The Internet, with a myriad of information at your fingertips, makes this the easiest part of your job hunt.

## Search the Company's Website

The company's website is where you will find information regarding their history, their mission statement, who the managers are, and what products or services they offer. Make sure to read the "About us" section on the site as it may give a little more information regarding the background of the company we well as the way the company runs and treats its employees. It may also be the area where the company states their work in the community, maybe they sponsor runs for different causes or go into high schools to try and recruit students for future jobs.

# Google

Google can be a great resource for you for anything you want to know about any company you are considering for a job. You can search for reviews of the company. People are always more than willing to post negative reviews of anything and anyone, so take that into consideration as you read them. But even negative reviews can help you determine the next step you take. Read them with an open mind and try to figure out if the person was angry or a disgruntled employee. Give those reviews less credence. However, if you see similar complaints from multiple people, maybe it is something you need to take into consideration.

Some reviews may be from previous and current employees, but you might also find some from customers. These are important in that customers have nothing to lose when posting a review about a company. Here again, read with an open mind as there are those customers who can never be pleased.

Look at what the company considers achievements. Have they won awards? Do they donate time and money to the community?

Some websites may list their investor information. If you want to know who is investing in this company or what organizations the company supports, this could be very beneficial to you. You can often also find information on the company's financial records. If possible, research these and see how the company is doing financially. Are they growing? Have sales decreased? Have sales increased?

## Better Business Bureau

The Better Business Bureau in your local area is an excellent option for researching a company. The Better Business Bureau is a reputable non-profit organization that fields complaints from anyone who has worked with a company in any way. They are there to protect the consumer. They rate companies in several areas and give grades from A+ to F. They rate companies on how trustworthy and reliable they are.

When you look up a company on the Better Business Bureau website you will find information on what type of company they are, how long they have been in business, the size of the company, how transparent they are in their business dealings, any complaints made against them, and how the company took care of, or didn't take care of, those complaints. Complaints are listed on the site for three years. You can see those by clicking on the "complaints" tab.

You can also find reviews by even more customers and employees. You will find positive ones as well as negative ones. If you don't see any reviews for the company, it may be that they are too new to have any interaction with others or simply that people have had no problems with the company at all.

## Social Media

Most companies today have some sort of social media outlets whether it be Twitter, Facebook, Instagram, or LinkedIn. These are places where you can find out what the company is really all about. Are their posts silly or professional? Neither type of posts is bad, just different. But then there are the posts and pictures that may give you a different feeling about the company altogether. What language do they use when posting? Are the pictures wholesome, giving the impression of a fun to work for company. Social media is often where people (and companies) relax a little bit and show their true selves more.

By checking social media, you can also take note of how often they post. Random posts here and there can show a couple of things. Number one, social media may not be their main advertising outlet. Number two, maybe no one specific is in charge of posting. Number three, when they post often and use those posts for their benefit, it shows that they care and are making an effort to reach out to those in the community and to new customers.

Another benefit of checking social media is that it allows you to see what contacts you have in common. LinkedIn is a great resource for this as it is more professional related. If you know someone within the company, you can chat with them casually about the job. Ask them their experiences, or maybe even have them give you a good reference before your interview. They can also give you tips on what the company looks for in an employee that could help you perform better during your interview. It could help you know what to say or what not to say.

# Competitors

Want to really impress the hiring manager? Know not only the company for whom you are interviewing but also the company's competitors. If you want a job in any industry you need to know it thoroughly. Looking to get hired with a shipping company? Know who the competitors are in your area. Know their strengths and weaknesses. Let your interviewer know why you would prefer to work with them over someone else.

# Job Ads

Watch the job ads either online or in the newspaper. If a company has a specific job listing for any length of time or seems to frequently re-list a job, you might want to ask yourself why. Are they having trouble filling the job because of lesser pay? Are people being hired and then quitting soon after because they found the company was not as it presented itself? Frequent job ads for the same position are a definite red flag.

Other questions you may want to know about the company is about their customer base, things they believe in, stand for, or support, and what the goal for the company is. You do not want to work for a company whose standards do not fit with yours. On the other hand, you may discover that you have a lot in common and can work together to help the community outside the confines of the office walls.

## In Summary

- Research the company online
- Research the company in person
- Research the company's business practices
- Research the company's competitors

# Chapter Seven

# TYPES OF INTERVIEWS

*"In most cases, the best strategy for a job interview is to be fairly honest, because the worst thing that can happen is that you won't get the job and will spend the rest of your life foraging for food in the wilderness and seeking shelter underneath a tree or the awning of a bowling alley that has gone out of business."*—Lemony Snicket, <u>Horseradish</u>

There are several types of interviews conducted today. There is the traditional one on one where you go into an office or meet at a restaurant and speak to a Human Resources or other company manager. These can range from informal to formal, depending on the company with whom you have applied for a job.

You may have to participate in a panel interview, which consists of you and at least a few employees of the company. Each representative from the company will more than likely have a specific job during the interview. One may ask the questions, one may show you around the building, one may just be there to observe. Do not think they are ganging up on you or trying to make you nervous. You want to find the right job for you, and they want to find the right employee for them.

Oftentimes interviews today are conducted online through Skype or over the phone. If this is the case for you, be sure to plan ahead accordingly. You will want everything around you to be quiet. You do not want your kids barging into the room telling you they need to go to the bathroom. Find a place in your home that you can make look the most professional. Do you have a home office you can use? If not, can you position yourself in front of a bookcase? Before the interview, take pictures of yourself seated in different locations around your home to see what looks the best. Wherever you choose, make sure that everything around you that might be seen on Skype is clean. Make sure you dress the part as well. Just because the interview is not in person, you still want to make a professional impression. Act the same way you would in a face to face interview. Dress appropriately. Pajamas are not appropriate clothing.

Let's talk a little more in depth about each type of interview you may encounter.

## Telephone Interview

There are really only a couple of reasons for a telephone interview. The first reason may be a screening interview. The hiring manager may call you after looking at your application and ask you a few brief questions to get you talking. This interaction will often allow the interviewer to make a determination if moving forward with your application is necessary.

The other reason for a telephone interview may be your location. Maybe your distance from the job place is too far to conduct an in-person interview. It may also be that you are applying for a remote position and meeting in person is not necessary. Speaking on the phone is sufficient.

Phone interviews can last anywhere from a few minutes to an hour or more depending on the job for which you are applying. When you do have a phone interview make sure you have a copy of your application and your resume in front of you to refer to if necessary. You may also want to have your computer screen up and the Internet open as sometimes the interviewer will want to send you emails. This way you can respond quickly. There may also be times they want to screen share to show you how to complete any other paperwork or to show you what the job entails.

Because the phone interview is blind, the interviewer cannot see your body language or your clothing, you will need to make sure that your speaking skills are that much stronger. Voice is the only tool you will have to make a good impression.

Make sure you are prepared for the interview as scheduled. Keep background noise to a minimum. Make every effort to not eat, drink, or chew gum during the phone interview as phone speakers make those noises that much louder.

## Skype Interview

Skype is becoming a popular way to conduct interviews. A lot of the reasons for a Skype interview are the same as for a phone interview – distance, remote position, etc. It gives interviewers a better sense of who you are than they could get from a simple telephone interview. Sometimes companies will use Skype for follow up interviews just to save time and money by not bringing a candidate into the office. But there are some different things to keep in mind for the Skype interview.

While you may not exactly like being viewed by video, a Skype interview eliminates a lot of stresses that could be caused by an in person interview. You do not have to worry about finding the location or getting there on time. Those things alone make a Skype interview worth it. But you still need to treat it in a professional manner.

If a Skype interview is requested, you need to make sure you download the software. It is free and simple. Do this at least a few days before the interview. See if any of your friends use Skype and do a test call. This allows you to see exactly how the program works so you will not look foolish on the day of the interview because you do not know how to answer or have not made sure your camera and microphone are on. If you are confident in how to use the software, that is a battle won.

When creating a profile on Skype, if you do not already have an account, make sure to use a name that appears professional. Many times people use silly names interacting with their friends, and that is fine…for friends. Just use your name or your first initial and your last name for the best results and easier searching for you by the company for whom you are interviewing.

When doing your test call that is the perfect opportunity to make sure that everything looks right to the viewer. Your friend can let you know if a mess stands out in the background or a light is putting off a glare that makes you difficult to see. There is a screen where you can see your face. Take a look at it. What is your facial expression? During your actual interview keep a pleasant look on your face. Smile. Act interested. Do not be playing with anything on your desk. Pay attention the same as you would if you were meeting in the same room.

Normally an interviewer will contact you; however, there will be times they request you call them. If that is the case, make sure to get their Skype contact information ahead of time so that you are not scrambling and sending emails at the last minute.

Just because the interview is online, do not neglect other things. Still dress appropriately, as if you were meeting in person. Have your resume and application handy in case you need to refer to it. Another good idea is to have paper and pen nearby in case you want to jot down some notes or questions pop into your mind that you want to ask.

It might be wise to take into consideration your Internet connection before the actual Skype interview. Using phones is so much a part of our society now, but they are not always appropriate. A wired connection to your Internet will be much more reliable than a data connection.

One last item to keep in mind when having a Skype interview is being aware of who else is home with you. If your spouse is home, make sure you give them a heads up that you do not want to be disturbed. If the kids are home, same thing. If you have a pet, make sure all his or her needs are met before getting on the computer. Close the door to your office if necessary to block out any unnecessary and distracting noises.

# Individual Interview

The individual interview is probably the most common and most widely used interview. The individual interview is normally a first step interview if there is no phone interview. This is where your outward appearance, your clothing, and you and your body language are the most important. More often than not this type of interview is one-on-one with a hiring manager or the human resources manager. The length of an individual interview varies. It can last anywhere from a few minutes to an hour or more depending on how in-depth the interviewer wants to go with a potential employee. The individual interview allows the manager to get a good impression of who you are and can usually tell by the end if you are the right person for the job.

During the individual interview you will be asked multiple questions about your skills and experiences, your past work experience, and why you think you are the right person for this job. You can find a list of possible questions in part two of this book along with answers for you to study and reasons for why a hiring manager may ask those particular questions to give you a better idea of how to respond.

# Group Interview

A group interview will involve several candidates for the job. Often in the group interview there may be minor tests to take and other screening options to give hiring managers a good idea quickly who the best candidates would be. After prescreening, hiring managers will then call back those candidates who did the best for further interviewing. In this type of interview a hiring manager can see those who separate themselves from the group and step out as a leader. They can see who works well with a team. They can see who works well under pressure.

In a group interview it is best to just stay calm, listen carefully, and do as requested. If you mess up on a test, don't panic. Simply move forward skipping over your mistake if there is not time to request help.

# Second Interview

The second interview is what everybody wants. This means that your first interview, whether a group interview, a phone interview, or an individual interview went well enough for the hiring manager to call you back and want to speak with you further. This second interview may last longer than your first one so you may want to double check as far as time constraints when scheduling to make sure that you are prepared.

The second interview is your chance to shine, especially if there are higher ups attending this interview than attended your first. Remember to always appear excited about the job, asking questions when necessary to show that you want to learn more. You may also want to bring paper and pen with you in case you need to take notes for any reason. Remember this is your last ditch effort to make an impression on those who have the power to hire.

## Panel Interview

A panel interview consists normally of one candidate and several employees from the company. Having a panel interview saves the company time when candidates would otherwise need to be interviewed by several members of the company. This also allows managers to discuss you after the interview and decide together as a team whether they believe you would be a good employee or not. Expect to be asked questions from different members of the panel not only in regard to the job you applied for but also in regard to their positions in the company.

## Lunch Interview

There may be times when a lunch interview is requested by the hiring manager. This is a more informal type of interview that allows the manager to get to know you on a more personal level out in public and not in the confines of an office. Restaurant interviews are more often than not a second interview. It is a much more personable and relaxed interview than an in office one-on-one interview. It may be one-on-one, but it also may be multiple employees from the company as well.

Since this is a more informal interview, this is a perfect opportunity for you to ask questions that you have about working for the company.

And just because they are paying for your lunch does not mean you should go crazy ordering. Order a reasonably priced meal that you know you can eat the entire portion at one sitting. It is never a good idea to go home from a lunch interview with a doggie bag. Try not to order anything that is overly messy. Remember your manners, as your mom would say. No elbows on the table, keep your napkin in your lap, don't talk with your mouth full, etc.

## Behavioral Interview

The behavioral interview is a relatively new tactic for hiring managers. It is a little harder to prepare for these types of questions as you never know exactly what they will ask. The behavioral interview is exactly what it sounds like. You will be judged on your behavior. The interviewer will ask you questions on how you would react, or have reacted in the past, in certain situations on the job. Think before you respond and remain calm. This is an area where you want to act like you are in control but also not be overconfident. The interviewer wants to see that you are a problem solver. This shows the interviewer how you will more than likely behave in a high stress or emergency situation on the job.

A few ideas they will be looking for in your answers are your creativity when searching for answers, your flexibility when things don't always go as planned, your ability to work with other team members, your tendency for organization, and that you can communicate under pressure.

As you respond to these types of questions, the hiring manager will want to know what the situation was, what your role in it, what action you took, and what the results of your actions were.

The reason interviewers ask these kinds of questions is because so many other questions can be answered with a simple yes or no. It is easy for a potential employee to answer questions with what a hiring manager wants to hear. Behavioral interview questions allow the manager to hear of past situations the interviewee has been in, how they worked it out, and how well they communicated the story. Real life examples can say a lot more about a potential employee than so many other things.

# In Summary

- Know what type of interview you are having
- Prepare for that particular type of interview
- Dress to impress whether they can see you or not

- Brush up on your communication skills, especially for those blind interviews
- Show them what you're made of

## Chapter Eight

# TAILORING YOUR INTERVIEW

*"When you know what a man wants you know who he is, and how to move him." — George R.R. Martin, <u>A Storm of Swords</u>*

B elieve it or not, there is a difference in interviewing with a large company over a small or startup company. Knowing these differences can help you succeed in achieving your employment goals. While some things will remain the same between both types of companies there will be some differences in how you answer the questions.

It is not necessarily better to work with a larger company over a smaller company or vice versa. It is simply just different. The job requirements may be different. You might end up with more responsibility in a smaller company with fewer employees over a larger company who can afford to pay more people. Employee relations might be different in smaller companies than larger companies. Within a smaller company you would have more opportunity to get to know your coworkers on a much more personal level.

A larger company may have more input into the community because they have more resources and more employees with which to work. That does not mean that a small company will have no interaction with the community at all. Some small companies do a great deal for the people that live around them.

Let's look at the difference a little more closely.

## Small Companies

A small company may be more family oriented than a larger company. If you want to feel like you are working with family members, a small company may be where you need to seek employment.

If you are interviewing with a small mom and pop company, chances are that the hiring manager is also the founder of the company. The founder of the company loves what he does. He has a huge stake in everything that goes on within the company. He is very passionate about what he does, and he wants to see that you have that same passion and drive.

When interviewing with a smaller company you may have to meet with managers from the different departments before a decision is made. More so in small companies, departments work together closely to complete projects. There may be departments, but they are all intertwined. You may also be required to work out of your designated department from time to time.

Training will vary from company to company of any size. Often with a smaller company you may get more personal training than you would with a larger company. Smaller companies have less money to invest in their employees so they want to make the best use of their time and efforts.

Pay rates may be more negotiable with a small company. Perhaps pay rates have not yet been established for your position. Small companies may be willing to pay an employee a little more than advertised if the potential employee can show they have the necessary skills and experience to make it worthwhile.

When interviewing with a smaller company, make sure to do your research as much as possible into their finances. You do not want to take a job only to lose it in a few months when the company declares bankruptcy.

Keep in mind that when you work for a smaller company you may be required to do more than simply the job for which you have applied. Smaller companies have a tendency to use more teamwork because of the number of employees. If you enjoy doing a lot of different jobs and trying different tasks, consider working for smaller company.

The environment in a smaller company may be much more casual than a larger one. If you like to work in a relaxed atmosphere, take that into consideration as you apply for jobs.

Smaller companies often make decisions quicker than larger companies. Perhaps that is because there are fewer people applying for the job or simply because they do not have the manpower to call you back for multiple interviews. In a smaller company you must put your best foot forward first because it may be your only chance.

Flexibility is a definite benefit of working with a smaller company. Some smaller companies will allow their employees to work from home, depending on the actual job of course. For jobs where computer work is the bulk of what is expected, working from home is sometimes an option. Smaller companies may also be more flexible when it comes to activities with your children, snow days when they can't go to school, and other activities they may be involved in. Do not take advantage of a smaller company just because they are more flexible with your schedule. You do not want to go into your interview and be demanding in the hours that you want to work or not work.

The insurance benefits that a smaller company offers may be considerably less than a larger company. The volume of employees makes it almost impossible to offer considerable, if any, health benefits.

## Large Company

If you just want to go into a business and do your job and not necessarily make any friends with whom you can hang out with outside of office hours, then a larger company may be the perfect fit for you.

When interviewing with a large company, you will more than likely meet and interview with the head of the department for which you applied. Yes, you may have to meet with other managers of the business, but the head of the department in question will have more to say in whether you are hired or not.

Larger companies will normally have training down to a science. They have been at it for a while. They know what works. They know it does not work. It may not be personal at all. They want to get interviewees in and out in an efficient manner.

Pay rates with a larger company be less negotiable. Often they have a set pay rate for different positions. They may be willing to raise your pay after a period of 30 days or so when they have been able to see you at work and know what you are capable of.

You may not have to worry about the bankruptcy of a larger company soon after you have been given the position, but still researching their financial state is much as you can is beneficial to you. You want to know that the company for whom you are interviewing is viable and profitable.

There may be more opportunity for advancement in a larger company over a smaller company. There are many more jobs to do, but they are spread out amongst more people. Often your job requirements will be very specialized so that you can focus on doing only what you were hired to do.

In a larger company, oftentimes the environment is much more formal. They may have casual Fridays or other days that are intended to boost the morale of the employees, but overall expect a more formal culture. Take that into consideration as you prepare for your interview with a large company.

If health benefits are part of the reason you were looking for a new job, a larger company may be more beneficial to you. They can offer you much more than a smaller company would be able to.

If you are looking for flexibility on the job, a large company may not be the place. Large companies have a lot of work to accomplish, and may not be as flexible with their schedules as you would like them to be. When interviewing with a large company, do not introduce yourself and then state all the upcoming dates that you need off due to activities with your children.

When you first interview with a large company you will more than likely meet with a human resources manager. The human resources manager's job is to weed out unsuitable applicants. Most of these questions will be generic as the manager just really wants to hit the highlights of your past job experiences, skills, and talents. It is more common with large companies to have initial group interviews and then if you make it through that round, you may meet with a specific manager or even have a panel interview. Whichever types of interviews you face a large company, expect more of them than you would with a small company.

# In Summary

- Examine the differences between small and large companies
- Look at pay rates
- Health benefits
- Interview process

## Chapter Nine

# TAKING A PRACTICE DRIVE

*"A driver reaches a destination by driving on that road, not by laying back to enjoy the view." - Nabil N. Jamal*

This may seem silly, but if you are in unfamiliar territory, it is a wonderful idea. People are often a little nervous before an interview and may get turned around while driving. GPS is handy to have, but it is not always correct. To make sure you will get to your interview on time and without issue, take a drive to the location, and if possible, at the same time of day as you will be driving there for the interview. This will help you take notice of the amount of traffic and the time it takes to drive there. This way, if there are discrepancies in directions or GPS mishaps, you will have these problems solved beforehand.

## Issues When Driving

Another issue may be construction. If there is construction happening on the route you originally planned on taking, then you obviously have to find another route. Waze is a great navigational app. It is constantly updated by drivers going your way. As you drive along using the app, you will receive notifications of debris in the road, accidents that are slowing down traffic, or any other obstacles that may prevent you from getting to your destination on time. If you do not have the Waze app, you may want to consider downloading it a couple of days before your interview and use it around town to get familiar with how it works.

If you do not want to depend on an app, print out directions before you leave the house. Printed directions are handy, especially if you lose cell service and your apps no longer work.

## Weather

Even after taking your practice drive, take note of the weather on the day of your interview. If it is raining or snowing, you will want to make sure you allow even more time than your practice drive showed you need. You can check the weather a day or so ahead of time to prepare yourself if necessary.

On the day of the interview, allow yourself a little extra time to make sure you arrive a few minutes early. This will give you time to fix any clothing or hair issues, go to the bathroom, as well as give you time to take a breath and calm yourself before what could be one of the most important moments of your life.

## In Summary

- Gain confidence by knowing where you are going ahead of the interview
- Download printed directions as well as putting the directions in your GPS
- Take a test drive
- Go the same time as your interview to watch for traffic flow

- Take note of construction or any other obstacles to reaching your destination on time

## Chapter Ten

# THE FOLLOW UP

*"Never let the phrase thank you stand naked and alone.' Thank you for being such a good customer.' 'Thank you for being so loving."* — Leil Lowndes, <u>How to Talk to Anyone: 92 Little Tricks for Big Success in Relationships</u>

You may be wondering if you should follow up after your interview. The answer to that question is a resounding yes. When you take the initiative to follow up after your interview it shows that you are serious about the job and that you are still interested. By sending a thank you to the hiring manager who interviewed you, you remind them of who you are as well as just letting them see a little gratefulness. Thankfulness can go a long way.

Sending a follow-up thank you letter or email could mean the difference between being hired or overlooked. If the competition is fierce between you and another candidate, a little thank you can push you over the top.

This is also a way that you can relay vital information that you feel is necessary for them to know when considering you for the position. Maybe you forgot to tell them about some of your past experiences that you think would help them lean toward you as an applicant.

There are several ways you can follow a thank you. You can do this by sending an old-fashioned letter, an email, or even a phone call.

## Sending a Letter

Sending a thank you letter in the mail may seem a little old-fashioned, but it is nonetheless appreciated by the receiver. Thank you letter shows that you appreciate the time a person took to do something for you or the time they spent with you.

If you have the address and the full name of the hiring manager or the person who interviewed you a handwritten letter is appropriate. Write out your letter as soon as you get home so that you can put it in the next day's mail. The interviewer will receive it within a couple of days, and that will put your name in front of his or her eyes as a reminder of who you are. This might make you stand out of the crowd of applicants.

If you are unsure of what to write, just keep it simple. Below is a sample of what you could write. Just make sure that you address the letter properly in professional business style.

*Dear Mr. Job:*

*I wanted to take the time to send you a letter of thanks for meeting with me yesterday and discussing the job opening you had available. I appreciate our conversation and how more much I was able to learn about the company on a different level.*

*I feel confident that I would be a great asset to your team because of my experiences in the workplace and in life in general. I know I would be able to fulfill all the job requirements effectively.*

*If you have any other questions or concerns or just need more information, feel free to contact me at any time.*

*I look forward to hopefully working with you in the near future.*

*Sincerely,*

*Jordan Smith*

## Send a Thank You Email

Sending a thank you email is not only polite but advantageous to you in your search for a job. Here again, this puts your name and face in front of the hiring manager. One thing that you want to make sure that you do besides thanking them for their time is to show your excitement for the job. This is also a prime opportunity to reinforce your skills that will prove to them that you are the right person for the job.

Remember that even though this is just an email, you still need to format it properly, use proper grammar, and complete sentences. You want to be professional all the way. Don't push send as soon as you finish typing. Walk away for a few minutes and then come back and reread your work. Make sure everything is correct and error free. Also, make sure you customize your email to make it more personal and specific to the job. Do not just use a template of the letter you might find online.

A sample thank you email might look like this:

*Dear Ms. Smith;*

*Thank you for taking time out of your very busy schedule to speak with me. I really do appreciate your time during the interview process.*

*After speaking with you I believe that I would be the perfect candidate to fill this position. I definitely have the technical and the analytical skills necessary to complete the job. I also look forward to the opportunity to learn more and to work with a team as that is not something I have in my current position.*

*Know that I am very interested in this position, and I look forward to hearing from you once you and your colleagues have made a final decision.*

*Thanks again for your time.*

*Sincerely,*

*Jordan Right*

# A Follow-Up Phone Call

A follow-up phone call is appropriate a few days after your interview. You do not want to call first thing the next asking if they have made a decision yet. You need to give them time to think and discuss things and consider all the applicants. However, a follow-up phone call does show you are still interested and that you hope to gain a position with this company.

There are definite advantages to making a phone call over sending an email or letter. First of all prospective employers can hear your tone of voice and can hear your enthusiasm about the job. Secondly, it allows you to ask additional questions if there was something you didn't understand or something you forgot to ask. When making a phone call your questions will usually get answered immediately. A follow-up phone call also gives them an opportunity to hear your communication skills over the phone. That could be very beneficial, especially if the job you are applying for requires you speak to customers over the phone.

When making a follow-up phone call plan to keep the conversation short. Introduce yourself to remind the hiring manager who you are, and then politely ask if they have filled the position yet.

If no one answers the phone and you are sent to voicemail, feel free to leave a message, but keep it short. No one wants to listen to a five-minute message on their voicemail or answering machine. Keep it short, sweet, and to the point. Thank them for taking their time to interview you, and then ask if they have made any decisions yet and let them know you are still very interested in the job. You may want to leave your phone number just in case they lost it or also just for easy further communication. Leave it at that and hang up.

***Are you enjoying this book? If so, I'd be really happy if you could leave a short review on Amazon, it means a lot to me! Thank you.***

## Chapter Eleven

# JOB INTERVIEW NO-NOS

*"A lot of us for instance are very good at our jobs but absolutely hopeless at job interviews"*— Karl Wiggins, <u>Wrong Planet - Searching for your Tribe</u>

There is a list of things you do not want to do when it comes to the job interview. A lot of them seem like common sense, but let's face it, not everyone has common sense. On the other hand, the issues might seem so small that we do not even give them a thought as we prepare. We all make mistakes without even realizing it. Let's take a look at some of these no-nos.

Do not be late. That sets the tone for the entire interview, and it is not a good one. By arriving late, you have made your first impression without even being seen. Always arrive early.

It is such a habit for most people to wander around life carrying water bottles. Bringing a water bottle, or any drink, into your interview is a bad idea. It just gives you one more thing to carry and can be distracting during the interview. You do not want to be drinking out of a clunky water bottle while the interviewer is asking questions of you.

If it is impossible for you to leave your cell phone in your car, put it in your bag or pocket after you have turned it off and forget about it. Do this before arriving at the interview. Checking emails and the all-important social media can be done before you get out of your car. Even if you have to wait a few minutes for your interview to begin, checking your cell phone makes you look bored and uninterested. Do not do that. And absolutely do not pull your phone out in the middle of the interview.

Make sure you know at least something about the job for which you have applied. Some people are so desperate for a job they randomly apply for everything that pops up. Digging into the position even just a little bit can help you determine whether it is a good fit for you or not. Do not waste a company's time by applying and showing up for an interview only to realize you don't want that job after all.

Make sure you submit a proper resume. Younger people may not have as much to add to their resumes as somebody with more work experience but a properly formatted and clear resume can say a lot about you. Do not give false information on your resume and state clearly the jobs that you have had and what your responsibilities were.

Some people have a habit of talking a lot, especially when they are a little bit nervous. If this is you, take note before the interview. Make it a point to answer the questions, but not take the chatter too far. A mouth can get a person into a lot of trouble. When we babble endlessly, sometimes we give too much information, information the interviewer can use against us. You may be making an impression you never intended to.

Pay attention. One of the signs that a person is uninterested in whoever is speaking is the fact that the eyes are wandering around the room or worse yet the person is yawning constantly. If this begins to happen in your interview you know the job is a lost cause for you. Go to bed at a decent hour the night before your interview. If the interview is in the afternoon and you need a little pick me up, drink some caffeine before going into the interview.

Don't trash talk. While you may know some past employees of the particular company for which you are being interviewed, do not say anything negative about them. Remember your mother's quote, "If you can't say anything nice, don't say anything at all." This was not only a good idea as a child; it is also a good idea as an adult.

Most importantly do not arrive at an interview completely unprepared. This book gives you all kinds of questions and sample interviews that you can study so that you know what to expect. This book also gives you tips on how to research the company and prepare yourself for the interview. Do it all. Be fully prepared and you will make a much better impression possibly getting that callback you so desire.

# PART TWO

*35 Interview Questions and Answer*

# KNOWING THE RIGHT ANSWERS

One of the most anxiety causing portions of an interview are the questions. One might hyperventilate anticipating questions they will not know how to answer. These questions are to help the interviewer decide if you are the right person for the job or not. You want to make sure they know you are. The 35 questions in this section of the book will help ease all your anxieties, at least as far as questions are concerned.

Some of these questions may seem basic to you, especially if you have had interviews before, but some of these are geared toward the person who is going out for their very first interview. For those with interviewing experience, do not look over those questions you think are too simple or redundant. Give them some serious thought and maybe come up with some new answers to help you land that coveted job that has eluded you thus far.

As you read through these questions and study them, do a little self-introspection. Think about how you got to where you are. Think about the job experiences that made you what you are today. Think about the things that you would change could you go back in time. Think about the things that would make your life better. Think about how you can go about achieving your goals. Those are the answers you want to be able to give in your interview.

# Practice Questions

# QUESTION 1: Tell me a little bit about yourself.

MEANING: This may seem more of a statement than a question, but it is one of the most important questions an interviewer can ask. It is often one of the first questions they ask, and it can help you set the tone for the interview and make a good impression.

HOW TO RESPOND: Think deeper than, "My name is John. I live in Alabama. I need a job, and hope I get this one." Tell them what your likes/hobbies are. Do you have a family? What do you like about the company, and what do you have in common? This is where your research of the company can come in handy.

POSSIBLE ANSWERS: "I have been married for 10 years. My wife and I have two kids who are both in school. As a family we enjoy hiking, camping, and pretty much anything outdoors. We destress on Sunday afternoons by taking bike rides on some of the local trails. I've noticed the company has some trails on the property available for employees to use. That would definitely be happening on my lunch break to decompress and finish the afternoon strong."

"Cooking is one of the things I enjoy most, next to eating. One of the things I enjoy doing every summer is cooking for our church youth group's camp. It's such a little thing for me, but they seem to really appreciate it. The times I enjoy the most are when one of the teens comes in after a meal to help clean up. We get to have some deep conversations."

## QUESTION 2: Why should we hire you instead of someone else?

MEANING: This is not a trick question. They want to know why you think you deserve the job.

HOW TO RESPOND: This is your opportunity to make yourself stand out among the other applicants. This is another place where your search on the company could be beneficial to you. Be specific in your details according to what you have discovered in your research.

POSSIBLE ANSWERS: "I have thought long and hard about where I want to work. I have researched your company a great deal and think it would be an excellent opportunity for both of us. I can bring in some of the ideas I've learned working elsewhere and apply them here."

"Honestly, I want to work for a company that looks outside of its four walls. One of the things that caught my eye when I was doing a little research on who you were was all your involvement in the community. I love that you support our schools. I love that you sponsor events to bring the community together. That is something that is definitely needed in today's society."

# QUESTION 3: What are your technical abilities?

MEANING: They want to know if you can do the job required of you.

HOW TO RESPOND: Honestly. If you are familiar with any technical aspects of the job, let them know. If you don't know something, let them know that as well. Show that you are willing to learn whatever it takes to do the job properly.

POSSIBLE ANSWERS: "I am proficient in Microsoft Word, Excel, Photoshop, etc. I learned some software programs in college, and I have kept up to date with them, buying new editions as they came out and playing with them to see what was new and different."

"I know how to run a welder (or other machinery necessary for the job). Because I have learned so much off of YouTube, I actually started my own channel to help others learn as well."

"I have been an editor for 20 years. I have worked with a major publisher in the past, working closely with authors, and preparing books for print. I have worked with traditional publishing houses as well as subsidy ones. It isn't unusual for me to work one on one with a new author to help them learn the ropes and get started in their own publishing career."

# QUESTION 4: What type of work environment do you prefer?

MEANING: The work environment is never a perfect world. Difficulties will come up. The employer wants to know if you can work outside of your comfort zone.

HOW TO RESPOND: Definitely give an answer to what your preferred work environment is, but do not stop there. Let the interviewer know that you understand we do not live in a perfect world where everything is just the way you want it all the time. You need to be able to work in spite of the environment.

POSSIBLE ANSWERS: "I prefer an environment that feels safe and secure. I want to work with a company, like yours, whose values are the same as mine. I value a welcoming environment for both employees and customers alike. However, I understand that things will not be to my liking all the time, and I will work around that."

"As silly as it sounds when a problem arises I visualize the answer in my head. If I can close my eyes for a minute and take a deep breath, it is incredibly helpful for me in resolving issues. After that, I carefully think about what the problem is and consider possible answers. Methodically working through each option, I eventually find the answer. Most of the time. There are times when I need to ask for help from others, but I hope I can be there for them when they have glitches. I prefer environments where we can work together as a team to get through something."

## QUESTION 5: How much interaction do you expect from your supervisor or boss?

MEANING: They want to know you can do your job without having someone stand over you.

HOW TO RESPOND: This is a perfect question for confidence. Show them that you will attempt to do all jobs, even if there is a problem. They want to know you are a self-motivator and a problem solver.

POSSIBLE ANSWERS: "A little interaction when I first begin working would be nice to show me how the company works and what is expected of me. After that, I plan on taking control of my position and doing it to the best of my ability. If a problem arises, I will try to come up with solutions on my own. If I can't, then I will go to a supervisor who might have answers for me."

"While I know it isn't always possible, I do like to see the higher ups down on our level, so to speak, every once in a while. I think that makes them more aware of what we are trying to do and what prevents us from completing our jobs at times. I think an informed boss is a great boss."

## QUESTION 6: Have you ever had to face a major obstacle in life or at work that you had to overcome?

MEANING: An employer does not need an employee that panics at the slightest bit of trouble. They want to make sure you won't cry or panic every time an issue of any sort comes up in the workplace. Sometimes things happen. Machines breakdown, deliveries are late, and there will be personality clashes.

HOW TO RESPOND: Be honest. Be confident. This is a prime opportunity to show who you are as a person. Tell them of a difficult time you may have had on a previous job. Briefly discuss the problem and your involvement in it. If others were involved in solving the problem, give that information as well. This shows you are a team player.

POSSIBLE ANSWERS: "A machine I was working on broke down. I had worked with that particular machine long enough to know a little something about troubleshooting. When what I knew did not resolve the problem, I Googled it. Sure enough, a couple of YouTube videos popped up. I was able to watch the videos and take care of the issue."

"We received an order of paper for a large print job we were under a quick deadline to fulfill. As soon as I touched the paper I knew it was not right. I contacted the ordering manager and double checked with him. We were able to return the paper, receive the correct paper, and fill the job order with the proper paper. My manager actually commended me for catching it before we printed a whole bunch of pamphlets we did not need and could not use."

## QUESTION 7: What qualifies you for this position?

MEANING: Do not get intimidated by this question. Also, do not get cocky. Employers really do want to know why you are the one they should hire. This is another prime opportunity for you to outline your skills and qualifications for the job. Your response can also show the interviewer that you have done your homework and know what kind of job you are looking for.

HOW TO RESPOND: State facts about why you are qualified for the job and that you are the one they should hire.

POSSIBLE ANSWERS: "I have received awards for web design. I have worked for companies as well as for myself. I listen to the requests of customers and follow their leads as to what exactly they want. I have never received a negative review from anyone I have worked with."

"I make it a priority to keep up with all the latest equipment/software in my field. I enjoy testing out new products, and that keeps me up to date. It also gives me new ideas with which we can work as a team."

## QUESTION 8: Is there something you have accomplished, whether on the job or outside of work, that you are proud of?

MEANING: An employer wants to see you confident in your choice of career. They also want to see a sense of accomplishment, what you have already done in a specific area.

HOW TO RESPOND: Do not get too caught up in trying to figure out what your greatest life accomplishment is. Instead, highlight at least a of couple areas in your life where you feel you have done well. If at all possible, choose areas that relate to the job for which you are applying.

POSSIBLE ANSWERS: "I have always loved working with children. I began working with the middle school youth group at our church when I was still in high school. A few of them were very disappointed when I had to leave because apparently I made an impact on them. That meant a lot to me and helped me decide I wanted to become a teacher."

"Finances are an area of my life I have conquered. After I got out of college I had a lot of debt. It got to a point where I knew I needed to do something and do something soon. I found a second job that I could do in my spare time at home. Every day I worked at it and in two years I was completely debt free. I'm never going back to living from paycheck to paycheck again."

# QUESTION 9: How do you overcome challenges?

MEANING: They want to know that you can take ownership of problems and be a problem solver.

HOW TO RESPOND: Here again, you want to relate your past challenges and successes to the job for which you are applying.

POSSIBLE ANSWERS: "I love a good challenge. In fact, I thrive on them. At home when I have time to relax, I enjoy working on puzzles. If there is an issue at work, I'll attack it like it's one of my puzzles at home. If I can't seem to complete the challenge myself, I enlist the help of coworkers and we will face it together."

"This was something I learned at my current job. Challenges are part of the day to day work. When I first started working there it was very frustrating to me. There were many days I thought about quitting. But then a fellow employee began showing me some of his tricks and training me in a new way of approaching those challenges. I learned a tremendous amount from him and will ever be grateful. The job, and all of its challenges, was not such a chore after that."

# QUESTION 10: What are some goals you have set for yourself?

MEANING: Most companies do not want to put time, money, and effort into training someone whose plans do not include this particular job. They want to know that you want to stay with them for the long haul. They also would like to know that your career goals intertwine with their business goals.

HOW TO RESPOND: Let them know how this job works into your future plans. Maybe state where you are now and where you would like to be in the near future.

POSSIBLE ANSWERS: "I think this job would be perfect for helping me gain knowledge in the field, especially in the field of marketing. That is an area where I am a little less knowledgeable, and I would love to change that. Given the history of this company, I feel it would be a great place for me to continue learning on top of completing my specific job tasks."

"On top of starting a new career for myself and learning as much about it as I can, I want a job that I can depend on to help support my family and me. I do have some debt I would like to pay off. I have set some personal financial goals as well as professional goals that I would like to reach in the next few years."

# QUESTION 11: How would you define hard work?

MEANING: This question can have multiple meanings. The obvious reason is that they want to know that you will be able to keep up with the requirements of the job for which you are applying. If you mention past employment, an interviewer can also determine if your personal and professional growth was stunted because of several factors.

HOW TO RESPOND: State how to make the best use of your time and the company's time. Talk about keeping at a job, even when the job is difficult. Show that you can be persistent in completing tasks.

POSSIBLE ANSWERS: "I know what it takes to get a job done, and I will work to succeed in that. I do not want anyone to have to go behind me and finish a task that should have already been done. I do not mind helping someone else with their work if I finish mine, but unless there are extenuating circumstances of why I have not completed my tasks, I do not want anyone to have to pick up my slack."

"I think working hard means more than just filling a quota for the day. I believe it means taking that extra step beyond the quota. For example, at my previous job I would often finish my list early and have about 30 minutes before I could clock out. Instead of checking personal emails as many of my coworkers did, I would use that as a chance to clean up my workspace. I made sure my orders were all in place, the floor swept, the trash can emptied, etc. I felt that was a much better use of my time and the time the company was paying me for."

## QUESTION 12: Can you show me some examples of your work?

MEANING: They want to see your past work, that you are capable of doing the work that will be requested of you, and that you do actually have the experience necessary for the job.

HOW TO RESPOND: If applicable to the job for which you are applying, create a portfolio ahead of time. Choose your best work that you are the most proud of. Also, choose a variety of work so the interviewer can see your range.

POSSIBLE ANSWERS: "I have put a folder of some of my projects together for you. I chose projects that were most directly related to what you are looking for, but I also included some other works to give you a better idea of what I have done and can do for you. There are before and after pictures and descriptions of each one. Feel free to browse through and ask any questions you might have about what I did."

"I thought you might want to see some of my work so I put together a list of websites I have worked on. I have also gathered a list of testimonials from previous customers. Many of them have included their phone numbers if you would like to call and speak to them in person."

# QUESTION 13: Are you a team player?

MEANING: There will be days when you will be required to work by yourself. The interviewer needs to know that you can step up to the task and be self-motivated. However, there will be times when you need to collaborate with other employees. Ideas will come from every direction and you will need to be able to sort them and work together to find the best ones for the particular job.

HOW TO RESPOND: Ambiguity is never a good trait to show during an interview, however, you do want to show that you can be depended on to do whatever work is necessary, whether you are working with a group or alone.

POSSIBLE ANSWERS: "I do not mind working by myself or with a team. There are times when I think one person is plenty for the job, but there are other times when I enjoy the input other people can give. I've worked with coworkers in the past who had great ideas when I could not think of any. As soon as they mentioned an idea, I was able to run with it and together we would complete the project."

"I have had both good and bad experiences working with teams. Often people share their ideas only to have them shot down by other members of the team. I do not think that is professional or productive. Encouragement can go a long way when working with a group of diverse people. I am thankful for both the good and bad experiences as they taught me how to deal with both."

# QUESTION 14: How would you pitch our company to a prospective buyer?

MEANING: Your interviewer can probably do this in his sleep. He or she wants to know you can too. Your answer to this question will show him or her how much research you have done on the company before the interview and how you can take the information you have gathered and sell it to a potential customer.

HOW TO RESPOND: If there is something you are unsure of, do not bring it up. Stick with what you know for sure about the company and make it look enticing.

POSSIBLE ANSWERS: "If I were to speak to a potential client, I would be friendly and show them important stats that make this company different from others. I would show them projects we have completed for past clients, and ensure them that we work closely with customers until they are completely happy with our work."

"When trying to gain a new customer I like it to be on a more personal level. I'll call someone on the phone instead of just sending an email. I might take them out to lunch as I feel that is a much more relaxed atmosphere. After finding out as much as I can about what their needs are, I would show them how your company can help. I would print out some information for them to see. Tangible items make it easier for a potential customer to see what can be done for them. Friendliness, although in professional form, almost always wins."

## QUESTION 15: What is your preferred working style?

MEANING: Your response to this question will be helpful for the interviewer in determining if you are a good fit for the company. If you have to have complete silence to work, yet are applying for a job in a noisy factory, they may decide you are not going to work out.

HOW TO RESPOND: Knowing what the job is that you have applied for will be extremely helpful in answering this question. All answers should relate directly to that specific job.

POSSIBLE ANSWERS: "I do prefer to work in at least a relatively quiet atmosphere; however, I know that is not always possible. I am able to get myself in the mindset of tuning out background noise and concentrating on the task at hand if necessary."

"I am an organized person, so I prefer my personal space to be clutter free. I can focus on the job better and accomplish more when I am not always looking for a tool I need or a report I can't find. When I do have to share a work space with others, I just have to adapt. It may not be what I like, but there is still a job to do."

## QUESTION 16: What are the unique skills you have that make you a good fit for the job?

MEANING: Part of the reasoning for this question is to make sure you understand the job and its requirements. You will want to thoroughly read through the job description before applying and attending the interview.

HOW TO RESPOND: Make sure you have done your research. You may have a lot of skills, but not all of them are suited to the job. Choose the skills you have that most apply to the job and highlight those.

POSSIBLE ANSWERS: "I was in Human Resources for ten years. In that time I was able to decipher what people were really writing on their applications and in their resumes. I also became a good reader of people in a moment. I would have an initial opinion of them before they even sat down in the chair. Of course, I did not base my hiring decisions solely on that first impression, but it did help me decide which questions to ask."

"Working with the public is something that comes easy to me. When I was in college I had to work the front desk at an office. My roommate had the job and hated it, but gave my name to her boss. I loved it. I enjoy speaking to customers and finding out about their lives. I remember details they tell me, and the next time I see them I can ask how everything is going in that specific regard. People appreciate it when they know someone has not only listened but remembered something that was important to them."

## QUESTION 17: What was it that interested you the most and made you apply for the job?

MEANING: Interviewers want to know if you did the research on the job to see if it is a good fit for you and your experiences.

HOW TO RESPOND: Many people are often desperate and apply for anything. That is not the impression you want to give. Show that you are legitimately interested in the job and do not be afraid to show some excitement about it.

POSSIBLE ANSWERS: "I decided I needed a change of pace. I have worked in the warehouse and on the line creating the products, but I would love to work more with the customers. Because of my knowledge in the details of creating the products, I can share with potential buyers more information than the average salesman."

"After having worked in the travel industry for so many years, I think I can be a beneficial addition to your company. My previous employer is retiring and closing the business. I've been following you on social media for quite some time now, and I feel that I can seamlessly move into your office and bring my clientele with me."

# QUESTION 18: Why do you want to leave your current employer?

MEANING: An employer wants to know what you hope to gain from working for him or her. Jumping from job to job and being wishy-washy about what you want to do with your life tells an interviewer a lot about you. Unfortunately, a lot of what you communicate here can affect your getting the job.

HOW TO RESPOND: Focus on the positive, not on the negative, even if your work experience was not the best.

POSSIBLE ANSWERS: "I want to work for a company that appreciates me as an employee. I want to be able to build up a customer base and keep them coming back for more."

"I am ready to face some new challenges. I feel as if I'm in a rut in my current job with no promotions available to me. I enjoy working hard and learning new things. At my current job I was hardly working, and I certainly was not learning anything new."

# QUESTION 19: What time do you like to get to work? Early? Right on time?

MEANING: Your answer will say a lot about you as a person. Your potential employer will want to know how committed you are to a job. Showing up on time is not a bad thing, but showing up early is better.

HOW TO RESPOND: If you are hired for the job, it will not take long for your employer to figure out if you come running in to work at the last minute or arrive a few minutes early. No one is perfect, so be truthful in your answer.

POSSIBLE ANSWERS: "Ideally I prefer to be a few minutes early to work. This allows me time to use the restroom, hang up my coat, deposit my lunch in the break room, and take a breath to prepare for my day. Normally this is not a problem for me, but occasionally there are extenuating circumstances, such as an accident and blocked traffic that may prevent me from being here on time. If that is the case, I will definitely call and let you know."

"Honestly, I have a tendency to run late. When I was in high school my mom set all my clocks ahead so I thought I was running really late, but with today's cell phones and technology, I can't do that. I have learned to tell myself that I have to be there 30 minutes earlier than I actually do. For some odd reason that works for me. Because of that, I usually end up at work right on time. I don't have much time to spare, but I'm not late."

## QUESTION 20: Is there something that we as an employer can help you improve on? A specific skill?

MEANING: A good employee is always willing to learn something new. This makes you dependable and indispensable when issues in the workplace arise. The more you know, the more the company will be able to utilize your talents.

HOW TO RESPOND: Be willing to learn. Do not show that you are completely against working outside of your particular area.

POSSIBLE ANSWERS: "I love learning new things. I feel that the more I know about a company the better I can meet their needs. For example, if someone is sick and cannot be at work I can step up and fill that person's shoes until he or she returns, that saves the company money in the long run. I want that dependable person to be me."

"Organization is not one of my best traits. I know you have a lot of work that comes and goes every day. I think the volume of work you have would help me to develop better organizational skills to get the jobs done to the best of my ability and in a reasonable amount of time."

# QUESTION 21: Have you ever messed up on the job?

MEANING: This is a question that focuses on your honesty and integrity.

HOW TO RESPOND: If you have made mistakes in the workplace, own it. Be humble when telling your story, but show that you learned from that mistake.

POSSIBLE ANSWERS: "I sure have! There was one time when I had to reset my welding machine to accommodate something for the next order. I was not paying as much attention as I should have been and didn't check my calculations, I misadjusted the machine. Over a hundred pieces had run before I realized my mistake. I immediately went to my boss, explained the situation, and requested that he take the cost out of my paycheck."

"One time I did not double check a book we were printing. It was a small book of poetry by a local author so I did not think it was a big deal. I was used to printing books and I only took a quick glance through it. Because I did not set up the page numbers correctly, everything was off. Fortunately, the author had only requested 50 copies so it was not too much of a loss for the company, but I still felt foolish. I always double check everything now. It may take a few extra minutes, but it is worth the effort."

# QUESTION 22: If you were given the opportunity to start your own business, what would you do?

MEANING: The interviewer is looking to find out what your true interests and hobbies are. They want to know what you value. Maybe they are looking for someone who needs to have a creative mind to fulfill the requirements of the job. This question shows how the potential employee would take care of finances if that is going to be a part of his job. Your answers can also show how quickly you can think in the moment.

HOW TO RESPOND: You will want your answers to be as specific as possible, even if it is not something you have thought about before.

POSSIBLE ANSWERS: "I would have to do a lot of research first to make sure the business would be viable. Of course, some of that money would go toward equipment and supplies, but I would also need to hire at least a couple of employees to start with. I would look for people who had the same heart and mindset as me with a love for the business as well."

"While I have never really thought about owning my own business, if I did have one, I would use it to help others. Maybe I would hire new single new moms and provide a nursery where they can keep their babies while they work. Some people turn their noses down at homeless people. I know some of them are where they are because of their own poor choices, but that's not the case for everyone. I might try to work with them to help get them on their feet and off the street. The homeschooling community is growing rapidly. A lot of homeschooling families have one full time income, and moms try to run a little business on the side. Maybe I could rent out booths to them so they could be making money with their products, but not always have to be there. That could be some kind of selling co-op of sorts. I am not really sure what type of business I would start, but I do know it would work itself into the community."

## QUESTION 23: For the most part, do you get along with your co-workers? Have you ever had problems with co-workers?

MEANING: Employers want their employees to be happy. However, no employer wants someone on the payroll who is difficult to get along with. Employees who cause problems within the workplace end up costing the company money whether through mistakes made on the floor or lawsuits filed by affected coworkers.

HOW TO RESPOND: Be truthful. Not everyone you meet in life will end up being your best friend.

POSSIBLE ANSWERS: "I am usually a pretty easy going person and do not have a lot of trouble getting along with my coworkers. In my experience, any time there have been issues, more often than not it was over a misunderstanding. I much prefer getting to the root of any problem with a coworker and working it out. When things fester, they have a tendency to be blown out of proportion."

"Yes, I did have an issue with one coworker on my last job. We were put into a team to come up with ideas on how to better train new recruits. I offered up an idea that was well received by the group. Later I found out that my coworker took all the credit for the idea and received a promotion where he could work with the trainees. I have to admit I was upset about it, but I did not say anything. I was not sure the issue was worth it. The trainees were getting what they needed and that was important. Then a couple of weeks later, my boss came to me and questioned me about what she now knew to be my idea. The gentleman who originally got the promotion was losing new hires quickly because he did not know what he was doing. Long story short, he was pulled from that position, and it was given to me."

## QUESTION 24: What would you do if a deadline was looming on a job and you were not sure you could finish it?

MEANING: Accuracy and promptness are an important part of any business. Of course, they want you to hand work in on time and be accurate.

HOW TO RESPOND: Things do not always run as smoothly as we would like, and at times deadlines are not met.

POSSIBLE ANSWERS: "Accuracy is key, but so is getting a job in on time. But, if I were in a position where I thought I was going to be late handing in a project, I would contact my boss and let him know. I would much rather hand in a project a day late than be on time and it be incorrect. Handing in an incorrect or incomplete project will only cost more time in the long run. It might be a little late, but at least I would not have to re-do the entire thing correcting errors."

"That's an easy answer. It's a lesson I learned in the past. There were times I would fool around and drag my feet on a project that needed to be done. I knew what the deadline was, and I was overconfident in my ability to throw something together quickly just before the deadline. Well, my overconfidence cost me. What I handed in was not acceptable to my boss or the customer. I was forced to re-do the entire project on my own time. When the next big project came up, my boss did not even look my way, in fact, he let me go. Since then, when I have received specs for a project I begin right away. I set daily goals, allowing a couple of extra days for mishaps or unforeseen circumstances. I have never been late on a project since that first time. Yes, I may have to tweak it a little bit to suit the customer's tastes, but nothing like having to rework the entire project."

## QUESTION 25: Do you think people like you?

MEANING: The answer to this question can show confidence or cockiness in yourself. It will also show how realistic you are.

HOW TO RESPOND: Be realistic. You know that everyone does not like you.

POSSIBLE ANSWERS: "I know I can't please everybody all the time. People are definitely entitled to their opinions about me whether those opinions are positive or negative. In the same way, I am not a huge fan of everyone I meet or work with, but I can separate my feelings for them to get a job done. My mom taught me that you have to learn to get along with all types of people."

"I think I'm a fairly easy going person. I can get along with almost everyone. Yes, there will be one that comes up from time to time that does not like me. I don't talk about them to anyone because that's when rumors start flying, which could cause further issues. If I notice that, I just avoid that person for the most part to prevent issues from arising. I am not one of those people who cries if someone doesn't like me. I'm okay with it."

## QUESTION 26: What is probably the biggest decision you have ever had to

## make, whether on the job or in your personal life?

MEANING: Your potential employer will want to know how you approach decision making, whether it is a big decision or a small one. By finding out details of that decision, they will discover how long it took you, how much thought you put into it, and whether you worked with someone else in making that decision.

HOW TO RESPOND: Show that you can prioritize when it comes to making decisions. Show that you can take an issue and all the facts surrounding it in order from least to greatest.

POSSIBLE ANSWERS: "I recently had to decide if I wanted to buy a house or not. I received a little bit of money from the death of a family member and wanted to do something worthwhile with it. I have been renting and feel that is just throwing my money away, and I want to be responsible with what I have. Interest rates are low. I could save even more money by living closer to work. I thought about it for a while and got the opinions of others before making a decision. I'm completely happy with the decision I made."

"There was one time when I was a training manager on a job. My responsibilities including hiring and firing when someone just couldn't do the job. There was one time I had a gentleman in a wheelchair who came in. He did okay with the work at first, but then his quotas started dropping and he started causing problems with some of the other employees. Those issues caused their work to suffer. Most of the other employees had been there for a good while, and I knew their work. As much as I hated to, I had to let that man go. He put up a fight about it saying he brought money into the company because it could be paid by hiring a handicapped person. That really did not matter to me if he could not do the job. The next day after I gave him his notice, he came in to talk with my boss when I was not there. My boss stood behind me and told the gentleman what I said went. It was hard to let him go, but I had to do what was best for the company and for the other employees."

## QUESTION 27: How are you at explaining complicated procedures?

MEANING: This question shows your communication skills, and also gauges a level of intelligence. If a person is good at communicating difficult procedures, especially if the person is applying for a leadership position, a clear answer can go a long way to helping a candidate land the job.

HOW TO RESPOND: Be enthusiastic. You do not want to start giving a boring list of instructions. Show some excitement and use terms everyone can understand. Analogies can be useful, especially if there is a lot of industry related vocabulary that is hard to understand.

POSSIBLE ANSWERS: "This is an area I excel in. I had one job where I had to train new recruits. I found myself saying the same thing over and over again. Sometimes there were sections I had to repeat because the new recruit did not understand what I was saying. Eventually, I had my training sessions tweaked perfectly and was able to explain all the aspects and procedures of the job quickly and efficiently so new employees would understand."

"I have found when trying to explain difficult procedures, pictures and text go a long way in helping new employees understand. I usually type out the instructions, with corresponding pictures, so they have something to reference while they are getting used to new things. Some people have come in and taken notes, but then they would miss something I was saying while they were writing, or I would have to stop talking while they were jotting something down. If I gave them a packet with all the information printed out, they could follow along and just stop to add clarifying notes to themselves once in a while. In my experience, that was a much better system for that particular job."

# QUESTION 28: Is there something you are looking forward to the most about this job?

MEANING: Your interviewer will want to know what is important to you as far as this particular job is concerned.

HOW TO RESPOND: After researching the position, state whatever it is you are looking forward to the most. Make sure your answer aligns with the job itself to show that you understand what the position is you are hoping to gain.

POSSIBLE ANSWERS: "I am looking forward to working with a new team of people. I have heard wonderful reviews about your company from past and current employees. This seems like an excellent company to work for. They care about the environment, the community, and they take care of those who work for them. I want to enjoy coming to work each day."

"This is a brand new company in our community. I grew up here, and know that jobs have been scarce. I think this company will be a great asset to those that call here home. I am looking forward to seeing the town grow and prosper. If I can be a part of making that happen, I will be extremely happy."

## QUESTION 29: What do you like to do when you are not working?

MEANING: Potential employers want to know what you are passionate about, what motivates you. Any creative outlets you have may be seen as an asset to the company. Also, they want to make sure they employ individuals who are well rounded.

HOW TO RESPOND: Share exactly what your interests are, especially if they show leadership abilities, persistence in training (physically and mentally), and working with a team.

POSSIBLE ANSWERS: "One of my hobbies is running. I ran track in high school and have continued it into adulthood. Running helps keep me in good health. It can also help relieve stress after a hard day's work. I enjoy running in several community events throughout the year that raise money for breast cancer and autism awareness. Those are a couple of things that have affected my family personally through the years. I want to feel that I can give back."

"I enjoy volunteering. Sometimes I go down to the local soup kitchen to help serve meals. We make helping others a family affair. My husband and I take the kids to the store and pick out a few things such as toiletries and some non-perishable food items. We have made deliveries to the retirement home, the pregnancy center, and just people we know that could use a pick me up. I always wanted my kids to see how good they have it compared to other people. It's important to me that they learn to give back. They love seeing people's smiling faces when they get a surprise delivery from us."

# QUESTION 30: What would your past supervisors/bosses say if I asked them about you?

MEANING: Your answers to this question show how you view your previous employers and how you relate to them.

HOW TO RESPOND: Even if there has been negativity in the past, downplay it. This is another area where you want to focus on the positive.

POSSIBLE ANSWERS: "I hope they would say that I was a good employee, that I was there whenever someone needed me to be. I want to be the kind of person people can count on when necessary. I don't want to be remembered as the person who was the first out the door after work every evening. I also do not want to be recalled as the person who only ever complained. I want to be the one who encourages others."

"My one supervisor would say she thought I was hopeless when I first began working for her. I don't know what the problem was, but I just could not wrap my mind around the job and what I needed to do. But she must have seen something in me that looked like potential because she kept working with me and eventually I became pretty successful in the position. I probably gave her a few gray hairs, but I sure appreciate her efforts with me."

# QUESTION 31: What do you consider your weaknesses?

MEANING: Your answer to this question shows that you are aware of flaws within yourself. It also shows that you are looking to better yourself. This is something that potential employers look at as a good trait.

HOW TO RESPOND: Yes, it can be awkward and maybe even embarrassing to admit to your weaknesses, but it is beneficial for you. Again, be honest in your answer. Start out with one of the main things you see as a weakness within you and then go on to explain how you have worked to overcome this issue.

POSSIBLE ANSWERS: "I do not always like to be around people. When someone comes to talk to me when I am busy, I know I have a tendency to have an irritated look on my face. I know I have put at least a few people off by this, and that certainly was not what I meant to do. I need to learn to relax a little bit and allow people to open up to me and share their ideas about work projects. When I do let people in, that is when I have come up with some of the best ideas. I definitely need to listen better."

"Saying 'no' is probably my greatest weakness. I want to do everything I can for the company I work for, but I realize overtaxing myself is not the way to do it. I would volunteer for every job that came across my desk. Working in teams made that easier, but it did not take long for me to become overwhelmed. Now, when I am asked to work on a project, I try to take a little bit of time to think about it, see how much I know about it already, and examine what I currently have on my plate. It is still hard for me, but I am learning to say 'no' when necessary. I think the rest of my work is better for it."

## QUESTION 32: What motivates you to work harder?

MEANING: This is another self-awareness question. The goal of companies is to make money, but it is much easier for them when their employees are happy and motivated to do the work without incidents. They also want to know that you are not high maintenance and do not need to be confirmed every step of the way.

HOW TO RESPOND: Be as specific as you possibly can. Maybe give an example from your past experiences of what has worked to keep you motivated.

POSSIBLE ANSWERS: "Personally, I just like to know that I have done a good job for myself. I need to do everything to the best of my ability for my own satisfaction. A thank you from a supervisor or a boss every now can go a long way as well."

"It is nice when the higher ups recognize those who do the work every once in a while. It does not need to be all the time, but a note in the paycheck, pizza for the team, seeing a boss out on the floor working alongside everyone else can be a great motivator for me."

## QUESTION 33: What are your greatest strengths?

MEANING: Knowing where a potential employee is strong can help with job placement.

HOW TO RESPOND: Share some of your truly strong points. If possible, keep them as closely related to the job for which you are applying as possible.

POSSIBLE ANSWERS: "I have been told that I am an encourager. I enjoy working together with my fellow employees to fulfill a job order. Working together and keeping the spirits of my coworkers up is something I think I am good at."

"I really enjoy working with the public. I do not have a problem starting a conversation with anyone. Once I begin talking to a customer, I find out what they are looking for, but also what it is that they truly need. Offering them suggestions that maybe they had not thought of before is helpful. I once had a customer that was stuck on blue draperies, but when I showed her a spec of her living room with other colors, she fell in love with something completely different. Seeing people happy with their homes when interior design is finished is one of my greatest joys."

## QUESTION 34: How have you gone above and beyond on your past jobs?

MEANING: Being proactive on the job and having a strong work ethic means a great deal to most any employer. An employee that does more than just the minimum required will always be valued.

HOW TO RESPOND: Show that you are not afraid of doing something that is outside your technical job description.

POSSIBLE ANSWERS: "There was one time we had a huge snowstorm. I have four-wheel drive and driving in snow is no problem for me. But, I worked at a hospital, which is a place where patients cannot just be left alone. I stayed and worked an entire extra day so nursing staff who were not comfortable driving in the snow did not have to come into work. It ended up being a fun day. I worked in pediatrics, and I and the staff that was there, brought snow in for the kids to play with. I do not mind going that extra mile now and then, especially when it can help fellow coworkers and make kids smile."

"One company I worked for kind of took a nose dive in the economy. Online buying and selling took away from our small business. The owner had to let a lot of people go, but I was one of the ones she kept. All of us had to spread ourselves out and do more work than we had been doing before. One of our jobs became cleaning the building including the bathrooms. It was not one of my favorite parts of the job, but I figured the owner could have let me go. I was thankful for the job, so I did what I could to make the best of it and show my appreciation for being there."

# QUESTION 35: Do you have any questions about the job?

MEANING: Your interviewer wants to know that you are clear about the job for which you are being considered. He or she also is sincere in knowing that all your questions have been answered. But they also want to know how well you listened. They want to see you thinking on the spot, which may be a part of the job.

HOW TO RESPOND: Be careful not to ask questions that have already been explained. This shows a lack of listening skills. For jobs where training is necessary, they do not want to have to repeat themselves to you because you were not listening. This is a question where you can show that you are excited about the job. Think about what you are really looking for in the job. Ask about extra-curricular activities the company takes part in, ask about learning opportunities for employees.

POSSIBLE ANSWERS: "I would love to know about your experiences with the company. How long have you been here? Have you enjoyed it?"

"I am very interested in getting this job. Is there anything you know of that I could do that would raise my chances of being hired? I would be willing to take a class or two if that would be beneficial to me and to the company."

# PART THREE

*Sample Interviews*

# Rocking the Interview

You too can be confident going into your interview as well as when you come out. To help you further in that confidence, this section contains a few complete sample interviews for you to study and emulate.

# INTERVIEW #1

Background Information:

Lisa is interviewing for a job with Interior Decorator, Janna. Janna's office is very comfortable and welcoming. The two ladies sit across from each other in matching wingback chairs. Lisa opts to sit toward the edge of her seat so as not to look overly comfortable in the chair.

Lisa does not have a ton of experience in interior design, however, during this interview she focuses on her strengths and offers up additional information that could be beneficial to Janna should she desire to hire her.

**Janna** (Company owner): Good morning, Lisa. Can I fix you a cup of tea or coffee before we get started?

**Lisa** (Applicant): A cup of tea would be wonderful. Just plain, please.

*Comment: If it helps relax you to have something in your hand, accept if they offer a drink. Taking a sip in between questions can give you that moment you need to think before speaking.*

**Janna**: Where did you hear that I was hiring?

**Lisa**: A friend of mine, Sarah. You had done some work for her a month or so ago. She was very impressed with what you did in her home. You happened to mention that your business was growing by leaps and bounds and that you would soon be looking for some help. My friend told me, knowing that I have enjoyed working in interior design in the past and was looking to get back into it again.

*Comment: Lisa is giving a lot of information here. She is showing that when she hears of something she wants, she goes for it. She did not wait for an ad to be posted in the paper or online, she took the initiative and made a phone call that could potentially change her career path.*

**Janna**: Yes, I remember her. She was great to work with. You mentioned that you had worked in interior design in the past. What exactly did you do?

**Lisa**: I was in college and needed a job that worked with my schedule. A local designer wanted help but only part time. I guess you could say we needed each other. My job consisted of a lot of running around picking up orders from local companies and delivering them to the job site. There were times I stayed in the office to answer the phone while she was in meetings with clients or working at their homes. I learned so much about design from her for the couple of years I worked there.

*Comment: Giving details of all her experiences is a good thing. Lisa is showing that she is not afraid of any kind of work no matter how menial it might seem. She is also showing that she could stay on the job for a good length of time while multitasking with school responsibilities.*

**Janna**: Why did you not continue working with her if you enjoyed it so much?

**Lisa**: As I said, I was in college and that was a few hours from home for me. When I graduated I had a job much closer to home, and I wanted to be near my family.

**Janna**: Have you dabbled in design at all since then?

**Lisa**: I have. I found some classes online that I took and enjoyed. I don't know how professional they were, but I learned a great deal. I also began collecting interior design books. They have given me great ideas that I have used when I bought my own house.

*Comment: Here Lisa is showing that she is always trying to learn new things and always open to new options for increasing her knowledge on the subject.*

**Janna**: Ah! A blank slate!

**Lisa**: It was so much fun! It was then that I began tossing around the idea of getting into interior design a little more seriously than just my own living room. That is about the time Sarah mentioned you to me. I looked your information up, called the office, and here we are.

**Janna**: When you think about your experience with interior design, what is the hardest thing for you?

**Lisa**: Matching up colors without a reference in my hand. I know what I want in my head, but I can't always execute it without a little help. I started collecting paint chips from the paint store to build up a color collection. I put the same sorts of colors on a ring that I can stick in my purse and carry with me to the fabric store when I need something specific. If I have a sample color in my hand, I'm fine matching things up. To just go by memory doesn't work for me.

*Comment: Lisa is being honest about her inabilities, but also being truthful about finding ways around that to complete the job.*

**Janna**: Sounds like you have come up with a way to take care of that problem. What do you think comes easiest for you when designing a room?

**Lisa**: I can see the overall picture in my head. I haven't worked with a lot of clients besides my family members, but when they tell me what their ideas are, I can visualize the completed room. I try to sketch out a picture or two and gather some color schemes so I know that we are on the same page.

*Comment: Here Lisa shows that she is willing to go above and beyond for customers to make sure that they will be happy when the job is done.*

**Janna**: Your resume says your current job is web design. Why do you want to step away from that?

**Lisa**: It's time for a change. I enjoy web design, but I feel as if I want to get away from a screen more and get out into the world and meet new people. Most of my clients now are all online. I want to get back to a job with a more personal touch. I can transfer a lot of what I know about web design to room design. Some of the aspects are similar as far as listening to what customers want, color schemes, what looks good, and what doesn't.

*Comment: Many people often want a change of jobs. Lisa does not state anything negative about her current job, but instead focuses on what she wants to accomplish and stays positive.*

**Janna**: If things work out and you are hired, I might be able to find you some extra work designing my website. I'm fairly technology challenged.

**Lisa**: That sounds good. I would enjoy doing that for you. It's something that comes easy to me. Having an updated website might help bring in even more work.

*Comment: Janna has noticed a potential bonus to hiring Lisa. Lisa gladly offers to do whatever is asked of her and use her talents and skills wherever necessary.*

**Janna**: Do you have reliable transportation? Some of the aspects of this job would require you to travel a little bit, just around town, but you might need to go to customers' homes from time to time.

**Lisa**: I bought a new SUV last year. I bought it for what I could haul in it. My husband and I enjoy going to flea markets and antique stores to see what goodies we can find to restore for our own home.

*Comment: Not only is Lisa answering the question, she is offering up more information about additional skills that might be an asset if she is hired.*

**Janna**: What kinds of things have you found?

**Lisa**: We buy furniture that needs a little TLC and restore it. Most of the pieces we keep for ourselves, but everyone once in a while we find a good deal we can't pass up, re-do it, and sell it.

**Janna**: That might be another area that could be useful in this position. Would you be willing to do that for me if a client wants something like that?

**Lisa**: Absolutely! I find restoring furniture relaxing and stress relieving, not that I get stressed a lot.

*Comment: Working with difficult customers can be stress-inducing. This statement is important to Janna in that Lisa will not get overwhelmed when difficult customers do arise.*

**Janna**: Would you be able to take a course at the community college if necessary to further your knowledge of interior design?

**Lisa**: If you thought it was important for what I needed to know I would.

*Comment: Lisa is willing to listen and take advice from people who are more knowledgeable than she is.*

**Janna**: Of course I would determine that later after watching you in action to see what knowledge you already have in regard to interior design. I know you said you designed your home, could you tell me a little more about the projects you worked on?

**Lisa**: Sure. We bought an older home that was previously owned by an older lady. Her health and financial situation did not allow her to keep up to date with repairs. There was a lot of work that needed to be done. We completely gutted the kitchen, taking out the wall that connected to the dining room to open everything up and make it more homey and welcoming. Since the house was older, I used period appropriate cabinetry and colors. It was fun doing the research for that. Up until then I didn't know how much colors had changed over time. I fell in love with the colors from the turn of the century as well as the furniture.

**Janna**: Do you have pictures?

**Lisa**: I wondered if you would ask, so I brought a folder along with me. I call it my brag book. I don't have kids, but I like to brag about all the work we've done on our house. The before photos are on the left, and the after are on the right.

*Comment: A portfolio, even if it's small, can speak volumes about your experience. If applicable to the job, bring something with you to showcase your experience in the field.*

**Janna**: Impressive! You did a great job. I love it! It looks like you have some natural talent.

**Lisa**: I don't know how natural it comes, but I do work hard to try and make things look the best they can. A little trial and error is how I learned most of my interior design tricks.

**Janna**: I already laid out the pay, the benefits, and the hours. Do you have any other questions for me?

**Lisa**: How many other people work in the office? I know sometimes when I get stuck on a problem I like to check with coworkers to see if they have any good ideas.

*Comment: This shows that Lisa enjoys working with a team and sees that they can be extremely beneficial personally and for the company.*

**Janna**: We are a small company. There are only four others besides myself. You would make six. I'm sure everyone would be willing to offer their opinions and expertise if you needed it. Thanks for coming in today. I'll look over all your paperwork one more time and give you a call either way within a day or two.

**Lisa**: Thanks so much for taking time out of your day to speak with me. I really appreciate it. Please let me know if you have any other questions or concerns.

*Comment: Lisa is showing that she is grateful for the opportunity and realizes that she just took time out of Janna's work day. She is also leaving herself open for more questions should something arise.*

# INTERVIEW #2

Background: Grayson is a recent Master's graduate. While he wants to take a little time off before finishing his PhD, he wants to use that time to keep extending his knowledge in his chosen field.

**Robert**: You must be Grayson. I'm Robert Smith. So good to see you today.

**Grayson**: Good to meet you as well.

*Comment: Grayson has been seated and stands to give Robert a firm handshake. This is a sign of respect and openness which can go a long way in an interview. Grayson also makes sure to make eye contact.*

**Robert**: Did you have any problems finding us?

*Comment: An interviewer will often start with small talk to help relax you before the actual interview starts. He or she might also use small talk before the interview to get some personal information and get a feel for your communication skills.*

**Grayson**: Absolutely not. The directions you sent with the interview preparation packet were perfect. Thank you so much for that.

**Robert**: Go ahead and have a seat. I'm sure you know that I'm the manager of the position for which you applied. I'm going to give me some information about the job and what will be expected of you during the training period. After that I'll ask you some questions to help me decide what your potential with our company is.

**Grayson**: Sounds good. I'm ready.

**Robert**: If you had the information packet I sent you I'm sure you saw that this was a two-year training program. Of course, you will be given your own responsibilities and projects from the start. You will be working closely with a senior advisor who can help you through your projects. Barring unforeseen circumstances, you should have the same advisor throughout your training period. When you have completed your training you will be eligible for senior management and will be able to work with mentees on your own.

*Comment: The hiring manager wants to see if the information package was read, and he wants to make sure that the potential employee understands what will be expected of him.*

**Grayson**: I sure did. That was one of the things that interested me most in the position. I appreciate the two-year training period as I hope to really develop my skills further.

**Robert**: Why don't you start by telling me a little bit about yourself and your experience in the field.

**Grayson**: Sure. I just finished my Master's degree, and I want to take a little bit of a break before working toward my doctorate. When I saw your ad for this position, I thought it would be a perfect opportunity to stay in the field, further my career, give me a break from school, yet still gain knowledge that will help me in receiving my doctorate. I wanted to gain relevant experience and use my time wisely. I am looking forward to showing you what I know and what I can do while still being in a learning environment. I truly think that I would be an asset to this company. I not only researched the position, but I also researched the company, and I don't think that there is a more perfect fit for me.

**Robert**: Can you give me specifics on why you think you're a good fit for the job?

*Comment: Robert is looking for genuine interest from Grayson in the job. He wants to make sure Grayson is not just saying what he thinks Robert wants to hear. Robert wants the answer to this question to be researched and well thought out.*

**Grayson**: During my work at school I found that working with a team is something I truly enjoyed. After looking at a couple of your projects and speaking to former and current employees I learned that teamwork is a big part of how you fulfill responsibilities and get things done here. I also think that I would have some unique skills to add. Just coming out of college I have a lot of new and updated ways of preparing projects for completion. I have learned a lot of procedures that make the job less complicated and finish it in a shorter amount of time. After speaking to one of your recruiters at a job fair and learning even more about the business, I knew it was the company I wanted to work for long term. I am confident I can move from college to this job seamlessly.

*Comment: Grayson is making sure the hiring manager knows that all of his skills are up to date and current with the latest research. He is also sharing that he is interested in working with a team which means he will probably get along with his coworkers.*

**Robert**: How familiar are you with social media outside of your personal use?

**Grayson**: I am extremely familiar with most social media sites. In college I belonged to the Service Community Club. One of my responsibilities, among other things, was to keep up with our social media sites. These sites not only kept the members informed on the activities we were taking part in also in letting the community know what we were doing. If we planned on helping update a playground at the park, often times members of the neighborhood would come on out and join us. Extra hands made the work go faster. I was responsible for keeping up with all social media so we could reach as many people as possible. It helped us attract attention from the newspaper and garner donations for future projects.

*Comment: It may seem like Grayson is giving unnecessary information here, but he is letting Robert know not only the information requested in the question, but also that he can multitask, be a leader, and put other people before himself.*

**Robert**: Sounds like you kept yourself busy!

**Grayson**: We were very busy, but I found the work extremely rewarding.

**Robert**: Can you walk me through a time when you had to communicate with others on the job?

*Comment: Robert wants specifics about Grayson's communication skills. While he may be able to communicate with people online, Robert needs to know Grayson can communicate in person just as well.*

**Grayson**: I once had a job working with a community theater. I was not in any of the productions but instead worked with public relations. Every year we had a big banquet for the actors, their families, and businesses that sponsored us throughout the year. I had to arrange everything. I found the venue, worked with the caterers, decorators, and special speakers. Everything needed to be coordinated and work together, and I was the liaison to do that. It was a lot to pull off, and I was only given a month to do it.

*Comment: This is a great answer to Robert's question. Grayson has shown that he can multitask, work with the public, and other businesses to get a job done. He has also proven that he can work on a deadline without getting stressed out under pressure. He also gave a number of details without being too long-winded but still gave specifics in response to the question.*

**Robert**: On your resume you indicated that you were instrumental in altering some of the training practices at a previous job. Could you tell me a little more about that?

**Grayson**: Sure. That was when I was in high school actually. I worked at a grocery store like so many of the other teens in the community. There were not a lot of job options. I had worked there for about a year when one of the supervisors had a meeting to ask what we liked and did not like about the job. He really did want to make his employees happy. One suggestion I had was to vamp up the training. I recalled that when I finished my training and was put to work by myself, I was really not prepared to tackle the job. I got through it by asking the advice of other coworkers, but I was positive that a more rigorous training would have been beneficial. The supervisor later asked me for more specifics, and I gave them. We worked together to come up with more ideas, tests, games, whatever was necessary to make training more thorough for future employees. Everyone hired after that seemed to adapt to the job much smoother and quicker.

*Comment: Grayson is showing that when asked a question, he can be truthful, but also respectful. He is showing that he notices when something is working and instead of complaining about it, helps to come up with a solution. This answer shows teamwork, leadership, and communication skills.*

**Robert**: Here's a scenario for you. You have a huge project due by the end of the day. Most of your team is out with the stomach flu. What do you do?

**Grayson**: Well, let's hope the stomach flu never happens. But, if I were in a situation where I was on a short deadline with circumstances beyond my control, I would do whatever I could to finish the project. I would meet with the team members who were not sick. I might even text or email the other members. I wouldn't want to call or Skype. Most people don't want to talk or be seen when they're sick, but they might be able to respond to text messages. Working together with whatever team I had left, we would get the job done. If I needed to stay a little later at work to do that, I would.

*Comment: Again, Grayson is showing that he does not get stressed out when difficulties come up. He is also confirming his desire to work together as a team, even if only a partial team, to finish a project.*

**Robert**: If I were to call your best friend, what would he say about you?

**Grayson**: I think he would tell you that I am hard working, reliable, and that I put my all into everything I do.

*Comment: This question can answer what Grayson's strengths are as seen through the eyes of another person.*

**Robert**: You seem to have a plethora of strengths, do you have any weaknesses?
*Comment: While Robert is phrasing the question in a bit of a humorous way, he honestly wants to know where Grayson thinks he needs improvement.*

**Grayson**: Organization. I can prioritize, but when it comes to organization, that is definitely where I am lacking a little bit. I realized it when I was out sick one time. A purchase order was on my desk and one of my colleagues needed it. He looked all over the place and could not find it because of the state my desk was in. After that, I learned to keep my work place clean and neat. That way I always know where everything is, and if I should be out of work for a day, I can easily tell someone else where to find something they need. Now organization at home…that still needs a little of my attention.

*Comment: Grayson is showing that he is not perfect and that he realizes he has flaws. He is also showing that he is working to overcome what he sees as failings to make his work experience, and the experiences of his coworkers, better. Being aware of a problem is half the battle.*

**Robert**: If you were a food, what would you be?

*Comment: Do not panic if an interviewer throws a completely random question into the mix. They presume you have prepared for many other questions, but want to know how you will react when thrown a curve ball.*

*There are no right or wrong answers to these questions; it is your response to them that they are watching for.*

**Grayson**: Let me think about that for a second. I would probably be pizza. I enjoy doing a lot of different things in life, at work and outside of work. I see those things as toppings. Toppings can be changed up and be different every time you order a pizza.

**Robert**: Good answer. I enjoy a good pizza every now and then. I think I just have one last question for you. Where do you see yourself a few years down the road?

**Grayson**: I would eventually like to settle down and get married and have a family. As I stated earlier, I want to finish my doctorate. I think the family will come after that. I don't want to neglect anyone who needs my attention. I plan on being here for at least two years to get through the training program. Depending on how much I enjoy it, I may want to continue working for you as a mentor to those who come behind me. I enjoy being able to teach people new things. It's kind of like when a child is able to put letters together for the first time and realize they have read a word. Their eyes light all up! The world is a new place for them after that. I want to see that on people I can help.

*Comment: Grayson gave personal, educational, and professional goals in one answer. He is definitely thinking long term with the company, which could be an asset to his interview and help set him apart from other applicants.*

**Robert**: I think I have covered everything I wanted to with you today. I want to thank you for coming in. We have several other applicants we will be speaking with in the next week or so. We will be notifying new hires after that.

**Grayson**: Thanks so much for giving me your time today. Please let me know if you have any other questions that I did not answer or did not answer sufficiently for you. My number is on my resume. I hope I hear back from you.

*Comment: Grayson wants Robert to know how much he is interested in the job, and that he is open to more questions or to another interview if necessary*

# INTERVIEW #3

Background: Short interviews can be information packed as well. But it is important that you get in the information you want your potential employer to know.

Don is currently employed at one investment firm but is looking to make a change due to lack of potential on the job and lack of interaction with coworkers. He makes comments about his strong points and keeps the interview on a positive and uplifting note. He never goes into negative details about his current work situation.

**Marjorie**: Good morning. I'm Marjorie, and I'll be conducting the interview today.

**Don**: Good morning.

*Comment: Don stands as she comes in the room as a sign of respect. First impressions are long lasting so make sure you make a good one.*

**Marjorie**: Thanks for coming in on such short notice. I looked over your resume last night and was impressed with your work experience.

**Don**: It was no problem at all. I actually appreciate you getting me in so quickly. I work just a few blocks down and my lunch break was the perfect time to come and see you. I'm excited about this job.

*Comment: Don shows that he is available and that getting this job is important to him. Also, politeness can go a long way as well.*

**Marjorie**: When I was glancing through your resume, it appears that you have been in this line of work for quite some time. Do you like it that much?

**Don**: Love it. I am not sure I can see myself doing anything else.

**Marjorie**: Can I ask why you are considering leaving one job for another when they are so similar? Are you having issues with your present employer?

**Don**: There aren't any issues except that I don't feel as if I'll move any further up or learn anything more. I am fairly stunted in my job growth there. We are expected to do our own work all by ourselves. Not that that's a bad thing, but sometimes interaction with coworkers would be nice.

*Comment: Don did not allow any negative feelings for his current employer to get in his way of this job. Potential employers see wanting to grow and learn as a good thing.*

**Marjorie**: Did you have any issues with the supervisors there?

**Don**: I did not. Most everyone was pleasant enough to work with. I actually learned a great deal from my current supervisor. He was always helpful. My only real issue is that pay raises were at a freeze and promotions were slow in coming. Even after working there for ten years and proving myself in the business, I didn't see me moving up in position at all.

*Comment: Again, even though the answer to this question could be construed as negative, Don does not bash anyone in his current office. He simply states facts about what he wants to improve for himself. Berating a current boss will make a potential employer wonder what a new employee would say about him or her if there were problems down the road.*

**Marjorie**: Do you have any idea of how much money you want to make in this position?

**Don**: When I saw the ad in the paper, I read it over carefully and saw what you were offering. That is comparable to what I make now. The ad also said you offered bonuses and those would actually result in a pay raise for me.

*Comment: If a hiring manager asks about your compensation requirements, make them clear. You don't want to waste their time and you do not want to waste yours if you can compromise somewhere close together.*

**Marjorie**: Can you tell me about some of the projects that you've worked on that you're proud of?

**Don**: Working other people's money can be a tricky and sensitive business, but I am proud to say that I have had clients who have sent me pictures of their new homes, boats, etc. that they were able to purchase from the funds they made after I helped them invest. Most of my clients are long term, and I am able to transfer my client list from one company to another without repercussions.

*Comment: This information will be beneficial to the interviewer. Not only has he had plenty of happy customers, but he is also able to bring a new customer base to the new company.*

**Marjorie**: What have you learned from working with your customers for so long?

**Don**: A lot. I have learned how to read people and deal with them individually. Each person has different needs. They have different amounts of money to invest, and they have different interests. Each of my clients is unique, and I had to learn to create unique portfolios for each one. Cookie cutter investing doesn't work. I try to get them involved in small talk to find out more about them, and then I can share my professional advice.

*Comment: In some professions, the client relationship is everything. Make sure the interviewer can see that you understand that. Be specific in saying how you work with customers.*

**Marjorie**: Again, I really appreciate you taking your lunch hour to come and talk with me. I know you probably need to get back to work. I have enjoyed our conversation and getting to know you a little bit more than just a resume. I'm pretty confident in your abilities, but I want to run you by my colleagues before I make you an offer.

Don: That sounds great. I have heard some wonderful things about your company. I think it's a place I could call home for a long time.

*Comment: Don is continuing to show his interest in working for this company. He is respecting Marjorie's decision to speak with her peers before making any decisions, but he also makes it evident that he is looking forward to speaking with her again.*

# THE WORKBOOK

In this section you will find 30 additional practice questions for you to think about and write out your own answers. This will be great preparation for your actual interview. Writing out the answers to these questions will help solidify them in your mind and allow you to recall them should a similar question be asked during the interview.

Use the lines, or a separate sheet of paper if necessary, to write out your answers so that you have as much space as possible to fully answer the questions. Remember it is best to write out more than you might need to say. It is much easier to eliminate information than it is to add in the moment.

## Questions About Teamwork:

1. How have you handled conflict with coworkers in the past?

   _____
   _____

2. Do you struggle in building relationships?

3. Can you recall a time where you had a dispute with a coworker and you wished you had handled it differently?

4. What would you do if you needed to get information about a project from a coworker

who was difficult to work with?

5. Do you enjoy spending time outside of work with your colleagues?

# Questions About Working with Customers

6. How would you go about making a good impression on a new customer?

7. Have you ever had to deal with a difficult client? How did you deal with it?

8. Have you ever had a customer come back because he or she was so happy with your service?

9. Do find it difficult to work with multiple clients at the same time?

10. Have you ever received a negative review from a customer?

## Questions About Managing Time

11. How do you handle multiple projects at a time?

12. Do always complete your daily to do lists at work?

13. Do you set goals to meet your work objectives?

14. How do you prioritize your work?

15. If you had a long-term project, how would you set goals to fulfill that project?

## Questions About Handling Stress

16. Tell me about a stressful time you had in the work place. What did you do?

17. Have you ever worked for a business that underwent a lot of change?

18. Have you ever had a job where you struggled to succeed?

19. How well do you think on your feet? Write about a time when you had to do exactly that.

20. Have you suffered any failures at work? How did you react to those failures?

___

## Questions About Motivation

21. What does it take to motivate you to do your job well?

___

22. Is there a time in your professional life when you wished you had done better? What would you have done differently?

23. Do you ever take the initiative to solve a problem or do a job even if it's not in your department?

24. Have you ever had to work while a supervisor was looking over your shoulder watching you? How did you handle that?

25. Was there ever a time when your boss gave you free creative reign on a project? Was that project successful? Explain.

## Questions About Communication Skills

26. Do you feel you have effective communication skills? Explain your answer.

27. Have you ever had a frustrated client who took longer to understand something? How did you deal with that?

28. Have you ever had to explain complicated procedures to fellow coworkers? How well did that go?

29. Do you feel you have the necessary persuasion techniques to sway people to see things your way?

30. Have you ever had to give a presentation? Was it successful?

# IN CONCLUSION

Hopefully this book has given you enough information and suggestions to help boost your confidence before that all-important job interview. The tools are here, and if you take advantage of them and put them into practice, you will definitely stand out among all the other applicants. Remember, application is the key to any successes.

In this book to have been given information about everything you need to know before you go to the interview. You have learned how to dress, you have learned how to research the company, and you have learned to decide what it is that you want out of life. You have been given questions to study and now you know how to answer them. You know what to take to an interview and what not to take. You know that you may face one or more of several types of interviews, and you should understand the differences between each of those interviews after reading this book.

All the tools that were promised at the beginning of this book have been given. You know everything you need to know to tackle even the most difficult of interviews. What will you do with the tools that you have been given?

I want to thank you for joining us on this journey to the job of your dreams. Knowing that this book has been helpful to you, please share it with all your job hunting friends and relatives. This book can be an important part of their job hunting repertoire as well.

Now go! Fill out those job applications and send in your resume. Get those interviews scheduled, show the world how to take control, and get the job!

# BONUS CONTENT

I wanted to add this section as a little bit of encouragement to you. So, your interview is over, and you do not know what to think. Here are some signs that your interview went well.

## Job Specifics

The more specific a hiring manager gets about the position, especially toward the end of the interview, tells you that he or she is considering you. Otherwise he would not waste his time.

## Second Interview

If the interviewer schedules you for a second one before you even leave, that is a good sign as well. She would know if she did not want to see you again.

## Pay Specifics

Again, the interviewer is not going to get into many specifics about the job if he or she is not interested in taking you further. When pay rates come up, take that as a good sign.

## Introductions

Did the hiring manager take the time to introduce you to other colleagues that were not part of the interview process? That is another good sign. That shows that you may be seeing these people again.

## Starting Date

If a potential employer asks when you would be able to begin work, that is a sign of a well done interview. If he was not interested in you it would not matter how soon you would be able to start working.

## Positive Affirmations

"You seem like you might be a good fit for this position." Take any positive affirmations as clues to the possibility that you may be soon employed. Hiring managers usually keep negative thoughts to themselves, but every once in a while a positive one will slip out.

## Time

Did your interview go longer than you were told it would? Human resource people are usually good readers of character. If they did not think you were suitable for the job, they would more than likely want to get you out of the office as soon as politely possible. By keeping you longer, that tells you he or she is looking for more information because they see capability in you.

## Other Opportunities

Sometimes an interviewer may ask if you have any other job opportunities. If they ask this toward the end of the interview, take that as a positive sign. Your answer to this tells them that someone else could be snatching you up if they do not act quickly enough.

They want to know what they are up against and what they might have to do to put you on their payroll.

## Body Language

The hiring manager was watching your body language all throughout the interview. (Hopefully you practiced what to do and what not to do!) After the interview you can take in their body language to read how well you did. Did they seem excited or quick to get the interview over with? Did they smile a lot?

## Bragging About the Company

If you found the interviewer bragging about the company, it was not necessarily because he is elated to work there–which is possible–it is because he wanted to make it look that much better to you. He wanted you to be excited about possibly working there as well.


If you noticed any of these signs in your interview, take heart! You may be receiving a call back. If there were positive things going on during your interview, you definitely want to make sure you follow up (see Chapter Ten) within a couple of days.

*If you enjoyed this book, please let me know your thoughts by leaving a short review on Amazon. Thank you!*

Made in the USA
Las Vegas, NV
11 May 2021